THE URBAN ELDERLY

THE URBAN ELDERLY

A Study of Life Satisfaction

Forrest J. Berghorn
Donna E. Schafer
Geoffrey H. Steere
Robert F. Wiseman

LandMark Studies

ALLANHELD, OSMUN Montclair   UNIVERSE BOOKS New York

ALLANHELD, OSMUN & CO. PUBLISHERS, INC.
19 Brunswick Road, Montclair, N.J. 07042

Published in the United States of America in 1978
by Allanheld, Osmun & Co. and by Universe Books
381 Park Avenue South, New York, N.Y. 10016

Main entry under title:

The Urban elderly.

    "LandMark studies."
    Bibliography: p. 171
    Includes index.
    1. Aged—United States—Social conditions.   I. Berghorn,
Forrest J., 1932–   II. Schafer, Donna E., joint author.   III.
Steere, Geoffrey H., joint author.   IV. Wiseman, Robert F.,
joint author.
HQ1064.U5U7   301.43′5′0973   77-84407
ISBN 0-87663-815-9

Printed in the United States of America

Preface

This book represents an attempt at synthesizing many aspects of the field of social gerontology that relate to the quality of life among older urban residents. While "quality of life" may be approached in several ways, this work focuses on the life satisfaction of elderly people. It presents the results of an intensive research effort designed to be comprehensive in its scope so that the complex interweaving of policy, social and other variables can be described and understood.

Studies of life satisfaction among older urban Americans are particularly needed. This need is accentuated by the facts that the older segment of our society is increasing at twice the rate of the population at large, and that the overwhelming majority of older Americans are city dwellers. A concern for the quality of life in later years touches not only the elderly but also government officials at all levels, academicians in the social and biological sciences, and many segments of the general population. For the most part, efforts of these groups focus on ameliorating specific problems confronting the elderly, such as poor health, declining mobility, poverty, and the like. Critical to these endeavors is the task of identifying and understanding the determinants of life satisfaction.

We have addressed our research report primarily to professionals, while striving for sufficient clarity to make our work accessible to others interested in social aspects of aging. We believe that researchers will find the study results provocative in that the influences on life satisfaction of familiar social and economic variables are viewed here from an holistic perspective. Policy makers hopefully will find new information about the determinants of life satisfaction which may be used to evaluate current programs and to develop new programs that might positively influence the quality of life among older Americans. Specialists in gerontology (particularly social gerontology), social psychology, human development, urban affairs, and urban social planning will find the book a useful study of the life experiences of an increasingly important part of our urban population. We have a special hope that those actually experiencing the impact of old age will find here a salutary portrait of their contemporaries.

We begin in Chapter 1 with a discussion of the problems of perceiving the "reality" of old age, and point to the theoretical orientation forming the background of this study. The following chapters are organized as much as possible to parallel the order of procedures often followed in social science research. In Chapter 2 we present a critical review of the salient literature in the field of life satisfaction. At the end of this review, we construct a theoretical model of life satisfaction of the elderly based on concepts that are identified in the life satisfaction studies. In Chapter 3 we operationalize the theoretical model by selecting variables from our data that are appropriate indicators of the concepts in the model. We next describe the sample of older people we are studying and the urban environment in which they reside. Also, we explain the interview survey which forms the basis of our analysis, and we discuss the techniques used in analyzing our data. Finally, we present a quantitative test of the operationalized theoretical model, and an initial view of the network of relationships among the variables leading to life satisfaction. Chapters 4 and 5 contain a description and interpretation of our findings. While Chapter 4 emphasizes those findings that pertain to a relatively personal dimension of life satisfaction, Chapter 5 stresses those findings that reflect an environmental dimension. The concluding chapter builds upon our research findings to suggest a theoretical perspective from which to view both the aging process and public policies affecting the quality of life for the urban elderly.

We would like to express our appreciation to the National

Institute of Mental Health for providing financial assistance (#R03MH27619) for an important segment of this project. A major component of our research was an interview survey which was supported by funds from Title III of the Older Americans Act; the funds were awarded by the Kansas State Division of Services for the Aging. In addition, we would like to thank the University of Kansas for providing assistance from its General Research Fund (#3807-5038).

We are also indebted to a number of individuals. The cooperation of Robert J. Leanna, then Director of the Kansas City, Kansas, Planning Department, was invaluable to the project. We also would like to thank William E. Henry for his thoughtful reading of the manuscript, and Linna Funk Place for her editorial advice. Finally, we appreciate the help we received from Ronald C. Naugle in the early stages of the project.

F.J.B.
D.E.S.
G.H.S.
R.F.W.
Lawrence, Kansas

Contents

Tables and Figures

Where are the songs of Spring? Ay, where are they?
Think not of them, Thou has thy music, too.

> —Keats, *To Autumn*

THE URBAN ELDERLY

ONE

The Experience of Aging: Varying Perceptions

In gathering material for this book, we have asked a large number of older people to tell us how they feel about growing old, what problems they have encountered and what satisfaction they have found in their later years. We have tried to remember that while our respondents are the "subjects" of a scholarly study, they also are individuals who can, and do, speak for themselves. If we listen, we find that they speak to us candidly, and at times poignantly, about their experiences. So as we proceed in our study of life satisfaction among the urban elderly, we will include some of their own thoughts to help us understand in personal terms what it means to grow old in this society. We can begin to understand the diversity in later life by examining a brief profile of four respondents, and their reflections on this universal imperative of growing old.*

Mrs. Mary Fremont is a 77-year-old black woman who has lived alone for twenty years. She rates her health as poor since she suffers from failing eyesight and emphysema. Her yearly income, which she receives from social security and welfare, is less than one thousand dollars. She does not attend church or any club activities. Mrs. Fremont has one brother who lives in the same metropolitan area, but she sees him infrequently. She rents an apartment in which she has lived for twenty years in an area of town where many older people live. She does not own an automobile but lives close

---

*Pseudonyms are used to preserve the anonymity of the respondents.

enough to services so that she can, and does, walk. She finds her neighborhood reasonably safe and attractive, and has a 70-year-old next-door neighbor with whom she visits every day.

> If I was young, I would take advantage of the opportunities offered. Although, in my time there was very little offered [for a black girl]. There is a lot of satisfaction, though, in knowing you have always tried to do your best. As the years go by, you have more experience so you live more fully each day. Minds grow. The most rewarding thing about my life now is doing what I can to help somebody else. There's really nothing I need to make my life better. I'm very satisfied. At this age, it doesn't take much for me.

Mr. Ed Jarvis is 85 years old and lives with his wife in a home that they own. He rates his health as poor and suffers from an ulcerated stomach and arthritis. He is a retired construction worker whose social security and pension amount to a yearly income of $3,348. He attends church once or twice a month and belongs to a fraternal lodge, although he attends meetings only on very special occasions. He gets together a few times a month with his brother who lives in the same metropolitan area, and he visits with his neighbors at least once a week. However, he would like to see more of relatives, friends and neighbors. When Mr. Jarvis needs to go somewhere, he must be given a ride because he is no longer able to drive a car. He does not feel safe in his neighborhood because he fears that he can no longer take care of himself due to his health.

> The best thing about life is having good health. I didn't think too much about it until I lost mine. If I had my health I could do some of the things I'd like to do. The most difficult thing about life is when you can't do things for yourself any more and when you don't have enough money to live on. Older people that are able can do some gardening or sewing, I suppose. But since I was 60, my health has been very poor. What I need now to make my life better is someone to take me out on pretty days sightseeing to kinda know what our town is doing.

Mrs. Gertrude Weiss is a 68-year-old widow who has lived alone for five years in a home that she owns. She describes her health as poor. She reports suffering from a hernia, arthritis of the spine, a kidney and bladder condition, glaucoma (she is blind in one eye), and an enlarged colon. She has had a hysterectomy, a slight stroke two years ago, and has poor circulation and diabetes. Her income, from her husband's railroad pension, is $1,488 per year. Mrs. Weiss does not attend church or club activities; and while she has three sons and two daughters living in the same metropolitan area, she sees them infrequently. She reports being disappointed in her children because they do not visit her often enough. Her most frequent visitor is a neighbor who lives across the street. When she goes to the grocery store, drug store, or doctor's office, she either takes the bus or someone gives her a ride. (She does not own an automobile and does not live close enough to these places to walk.) While she finds her neighborhood attractive and likes her neighbors, she feels that she would be better off living in an apartment complex for senior citizens.

> If I had my life to live over again, I wouldn't have children and I would try to get a better education. The best thing about my life was marriage to my husband. He was sick so long and never complained. He worked hard to support his family. It's difficult now being a widow and living alone. I was very contented with my husband. He was a good man. I miss him very much. Since I was 60, I have lost my husband and I have developed several ailments that I will have the rest of my life. The most satisfying thing in my life now is just trying to keep up my home. The thing that I need the most in my life now is companionship, not being alone almost 24 hours a day. I also need more income because my health costs are so much I hardly have enough for groceries.

Mr. John Clarke is 67 years old and lives with his 73-year-old wife in their own home. He feels that he is in fairly good health although he is slightly deaf and suffered a heart attack a few years ago. Mr. Clarke was employed as an auto worker and retired because of his age. His yearly income of $5,400 comes from social security and a pension. He does not attend church or club meetings, but he is very active in his garden and subscribes to several gardening magazines. He visits with a sister living in the same community and gets together with friends at least once a week. When he needs to go somewhere, he drives his own car. He likes his neighbors and his neighborhood which he finds both safe and attractive.

Getting married was the most rewarding thing in my life. Working on a job also gave me satisfaction. We always managed, my wife and me, but the most difficult time for us was when we lived in the Ozarks during the Depression. After I was 60, I quit work. I enjoy not having to get up at 4 a.m. It's good to be able to do what you want to do and when you want to do it. I've done more fishing, had more time for other things. I work in my garden in summer. When the weather is nice I work outdoors in the winter too. I can't think of anything I need to make my life better. I'm as happy as I can be. I have good health, I enjoy my hobbies and activities, and we have plenty of income.

What do the experiences of these four people tell us about the conditions that make for a satisfying life? The experience of Mr. Clarke, who is quite satisfied, would suggest that an adequate income, owning an automobile, having an active interest in a hobby, contacts with relatives, a pleasant neighborhood, interaction with friends and neighbors, and good health all combine to produce a high level of life satisfaction. Yet Mrs. Fremont, who also reports satisfaction and contentment, has a meager income, does not own an automobile, reports no hobbies, and rarely sees her only relative. Both report that they are pleased with their neighborhoods and have frequent contact with their neighbors; but so does Mrs. Weiss who is not satisfied with her life. Mr. Jarvis complains of ill health, while Mr. Clarke and Mrs. Fremont do not perceive their health as a problem. Yet he has suffered a heart attack and is partially deaf; she has emphysema and is partially blind. Mrs. Weiss, who has the largest number of health problems, speaks more of loneliness. At the same time, Mrs. Fremont, who is also a widow, does not identify loneliness as a problem.

These four vignettes reveal quite different pictures of life satisfaction in old age. Mr. Jarvis's experiences are punctuated by diminished capacity and failing health, while Mrs. Weiss suffers from loneliness, illness and an increasingly inadequate income. Mrs. Fremont, on the other hand, provides us with a portrait of serenity accented by feelings of a job well done; and Mr. Clarke's experience suggests that the satisfying life comes from a lively interest in hobbies that is made possible by leisure time and the release from the demands of a job.

Does one of these represent the true picture of life satisfaction among older city dwellers, while the others are merely aberrations?

Any researcher concerned with such a question is faced with recognizing the complexities and ambiguities of attempting to conceptualize what the "reality" of life satisfaction or morale is. Havighurst's and Albrecht's 1953 comment is still relevant: "Nobody has yet succeeded in measuring happiness with assured accuracy, but this must not prevent us from asking and trying to answer the question."[1] In Chapter 2 we review seminal investigations of life experiences thought to be the determinants of life satisfaction and indicate our preferred conceptualization of the term. At this point, however, we wish merely to point to the perceptual uncertainties in establishing the "reality" of life satisfaction.

The instruments of observation brought to bear on any phenomenon are, of course, crucial to characterizing its reality. Tibbitts' synthesis of major efforts to observe morale, that is, life satisfaction, suggests the plethora of questions which may arise.[2] In determining life satisfaction should one use, for example, long structured interviews, in-depth unstructured interviews, or Thematic Apperception Test cards—or some combination of these instruments, as Cumming, *et al.*, did in 1958? How does one integrate the data from these instruments when the categories of each instrument are not similar? Should one derive measurement of attitudes as well as behaviors, and, if so, which activities are relevant and how should they be weighted vis-a-vis attitudes?[3] Can one usefully invoke and combine scales developed by different researchers working on similar general problems (e.g., Kutner's 1956 scale of subjective estimates of personal morale,[4] and Srole's 1956 scale of individual's perceptions of aspects of the social order and personal "anomie"[5]) even when the scales are measuring somewhat disparate attitudes? If one uses interviewers' subjective rankings of respondents' morale, what elements are involved in arriving at such subjective rankings? These are some of the salient questions that have been raised in the course of the scholarly discernment of life satisfaction. We address these questions and related procedural issues at various points in Chapters 2 and 3.

A further aspect of the elusive nature of morale is its changing character during the life cycle. That is, degree of life satisfaction may vary in a pattern of peaks and valleys—not of steady decline— throughout the life cycle, with varying circumstances surrounding those peaks and valleys.[6] If so, and if different age groups have different needs for support (e.g., disparate needs for intergenerational ties of familial affection),[7] this suggests a source of possible intergenerational strains that could adversely affect the morale of the elderly under some circumstances.

At this point we might pause to ask ourselves the more philosophical question: Is high morale a goal that one should reasonably expect to achieve, and, if achievable, is it desirable for older people or anyone else? We can imagine some other cultures, or perhaps some groups within our own society, that for religious or other reasons expect, and indeed desire, worldly suffering. There are also many people who do not desire adversity, but who feel it is unreasonable to expect continuing happiness. However, the broad impulse in contemporary American culture is to value happiness. The maturation of the American industrial economy in the late nineteenth and early twentieth centuries extended the limits of our imagined possibilities with respect to the living standards of all our citizens and raised individual expectations to unprecedented heights. Consequently, Americans place a premium on achieving and maintaining high morale, even when circumstances do not justify such expectations. Given this general cultural setting, it is a rare individual who is not convinced that personal satisfaction (self-respect, contentment, happiness) is the logical outcome of a lifetime of hard work and good citizenship. On the other hand, these cultural proclivities may create a dilemma for some individuals. Since socially created expectations can be unrealistically high, some people may be forced to lower them considerably in order to maintain high morale. This would apply to many groups in American society, but it may bear particularly on older individuals who often find it increasingly difficult to satisfy the expectations of their earlier years.

To help clarify the nature and dynamics of life satisfaction, we are devoting this book to the study of people 60 years of age and older who live in a city not unlike cities across the county. The study area, Kansas City, Kansas, is part of the metropolitan area which also includes Kansas City, Missouri. (This latter city was the locus of a series of studies in the 1950s—the Kansas City studies—discussed further in Chapter 2.)

The elderly have only recently been in the limelight, as a result of their having organized to some extent and thereby gained a measure of political recognition as a separate group in the nation. Nevertheless, despite our greater awareness of the elderly, there is keen sensitivity among professional students of aging and the beginnings of understanding among the lay public that our knowledge of old age has been far from adequate and that there is need for extending that knowledge.

It is becoming clear that a number of social characteristics often thought typical of elderly people—we will call them folk beliefs—do not coincide with self-reported experiences of old people, as shown in systematic research. It seems at present there are perhaps two social gerontological "realities": one constituted of well-established folk beliefs; and another less secure and emerging "reality" derived from social scientific research into the self-reported personal experiences of the elderly.

Both "realities" are "true" in that they can help people organize and cope with data about elderly people's experience. The folk beliefs are eminently practical in that they are the props of a consensus reality, according to which there can be agreement—often tacit and often shared by both young and old—about what the elderly are like, what they feel, how they behave, and how one can or should respond to them. Such beliefs are "true" because people take them to be so.[8] Yet, practical and "true" as the folk beliefs about old people are, some of them prove troublesome, for the same reason that folk beliefs about other populations are troublesome, i.e., beliefs may be at variance with the self-reported personal experience of the people in question. Thus, folk beliefs contribute to maltreatment of human groups, and they contribute to general bewilderment when members of groups do not behave in ways we would have predicted on the basis of the folk assumptions about them. Thus, such beliefs can breed general mystification about the experiences of our fellow human beings, and in the process everyone may suffer. One of the most harmful consequences is that people in minority groups (among which the elderly are the fastest growing) tend to accept negative stereotypes about experiences of members of their own group, even when their own experience contradicts those stereotypes.

What *are* the principal items in the American folk philosophy about old age which work so actively upon us? They seem to break down into three rough groupings: one made up of general views about old age; another of negative images of the elderly; and a third which romanticizes the experience of old age.

In the first category, a general view of old age is that older people are a homogeneous group and have a uniform set of experiences. As our vignettes and such studies as Harris' and Gubrium's indicate, old people have at their disposal differing amounts of money or other economic resources, have different feelings of sel-worth, interact with friends and neighbors with varying degrees of frequency and closeness, belong to differing social classes, and live in diverse housing conditions. Thus elderly people and their experiences of old age are diverse.[9] A major problem which stems from ignoring the diversity of older people's experience is that it might suggest that they live in a social vacuum. "The problem with [a uniform] image of the elderly . . . is that it ignores social constraints on the lives of aged persons. It assumes that persons are individuals, that such persons do have complete control over their lives, and that such control is rationally manipulated to gain various ends."[10] One might assume easily that an old person's failure to achieve such control should be attributed only to his or her own ineptitude or moral failing.

To the extent that Americans see old people in this way, it is but a special application to the elderly of a generalized view that Americans have of themselves, according to anthropologist Edward Hall. He suggests that Americans assume that failures in desired behavior derive from an individual's personal weakness, rather than from weakness in the support "props" of the society. "Americans have come to hold the view," says Hall, "that the controls exist in the person and not in the situation."[11] The consequence of this assumption, then, is a tendency to place the blame for failure on the individual and to ignore contributing social factors. Gubrium writes about the inadequacy of this view vis-a-vis the elderly by emphasizing certain important features of social life impacting on the behavior of old people, such as public expectations (which may differ from one situation to another) and physical limitations in the social setting of an old person's daily life.[12]

Another general belief suggests that becoming an old person is a clearly marked, perhaps sudden experience, like graduating from high school or becoming a parent. According to this view, one would be young at age 64 and at 65 an "old timer." Framed this way, the notion appears rigid and absurd. Personal experience and systematic studies contradict the idea that old age happens suddenly. These show instead that people continue to "be themselves" by maintaining rather consistent goals and ways of reaching them throughout their lives, and that people do not become senior citizens precipitously at any one point.[13] This suggests the limitation of another folk belief about aging in our society, namely that age itself—the mere accumulation of years—is the most significant factor in the process of becoming a senior citizen, and that the fact of age creates serious problems for these people. Certainly, older people do share with each other their chronological age, but a myriad of factors impinge on the various ways any given point of chronology is viewed and experienced by a person.

A second category of ideas about the elderly are mostly negative ones about the physical, social, and psychological conditions presumed to characterize that group. Such ideas gain prominence from newspaper and magazine pieces which emphasize the sick, socially isolated, abandoned, and thoroughly miserable condition of the elderly. Some books produce the same impression. As a case in point, a recently published book opens with a portrait—billed as "an only too accurate account of a retirement dream turned nightmare"—of a woman living by herself in a Florida motel room where she is ill, pinched by poverty, lonely, and gnawed by anxieties.[14] The authors contrast this woman's plight with practices of primitive Bolivians (who left their old behind as they pressed on with their nomadic food quest), of certain American Indian tribes (who abandoned their old to die in special huts), and of the Eskimos (who left their aged in snowbanks, on ice flows, or forced them to paddle off on one-way kayak trips to sea). The authors then ask rhetorically whether Americans treat their enfeebled old any better. Their answer is clearly intended to be negative.

Before accepting a perhaps too-grim picture of American old age, it is worthwhile looking at some of the central ideas that go into the negative folk philosophy. To begin with, there is the notion that old people as a group are poor and suffer thereby in a way that is distinctive from younger people. In fact, the elderly *are* poorer than younger people; the median household income of those under 65 is $12,000, whereas it is $4,800 for those 65 and over. But there is evidence suggesting that the low-income elderly are less troubled by their economic status than the low-income young, because the elderly support fewer dependents and have fewer needs and/or expectations.[15] The effect of poverty should not be discounted, but the elderly population at large is not properly viewed as miserably poor. Nevertheless, a popular belief to that effect is suggested by data indicating that only a small percentage (15 percent) of the elderly feel inadequate funds is a very serious problem, while 62 percent of the public assume inadequate funds is a very serious problem for the elderly.[16]

What about the health of the aged? Again the public image is worse than the apparent reality. Twenty-one percent of those 65 and over report that "poor health" is a very serious problem for them personally, while 51 percent of the public think that "poor health" is a very serious problem to most of the over-65 population.[17] A similarly exaggerated picture of the medical plight of old people pertains to the public image of medical care for the elderly. Ten percent of the over-65 population claim "not enough medical care" is a very serious problem for them, whereas 44 percent of the public felt that "not enough medical care" was a very serious problem for most of the elderly.[18] Again, we find a wide gap between public expectation and self-reported experience with regard to the loneliness of older people. Sixty percent of the public believe that, for most of the aged, loneliness is a very serious problem. But only 12 percent of people 65 and over said that they felt that loneliness was a very serious personal problem.[19] From these brief citations alone it would seem that negative aspects of old age in our country have been exaggerated. This conclusion is further underscored by data indicating that the elderly subjectively do not view their general fate as any more adverse than younger people (18–64) view their own.[20]

This information tends, then, to call into question the validity of the ideas undergirding the popular negative view of American old age. It also suggests that there is more of continuity than discontinuity in the progression from youth to middle age to old age. If so, people may have less to fear from progressing in the life cycle than they expect. It may be that the "great shock of the future, as it creeps up upon us in simple tomorrows, is likely to be how much it manages to resemble yesterday."[21]

Clearly, however, there is an active negative component to the folk philosophy at work among the American public. It impacts on both the old and young. One of the most striking findings in the Harris study is that people 18–64 and 64-and-older are in substantial agreement about the problems of most people over 65. In other words, the elderly too have incorporated the folk philosophy of old age. "They apparently assume that life is really tough for most people over 65 and that they are merely exceptions to the rule."[22] As an example of this assumption, one of our elderly respondents comments, "There's nothing that I need to make my own life better. But there's so many other older people that do need help, that don't have a family and friends and neighbors like mine." That both young and old can subscribe to an exaggerated negative view of old age, even when one's own experience contradicts that negative view, suggests the presence in society of an unwarranted fear of growing old. Certainly, advancing age can be associated with the decline of some faculties. However, everyday observation and research findings indicate that many characteristics need not decline or, at least, need not decline precipitously or uniformly among the aged population. Indeed, some faculties may be enhanced by the experience of growing old. Clearly, then, Americans view old age with a selective focus. This selection is based on the characteristics Americans value most highly. That is, we are preoccupied with such characteristics as independence, productivity, health, and physical strength. These attributes are more susceptible to decline in old age than less valued personal traits such as serenity, folk wisdom, and altruism. In this context, aging presents a threat to the value system and, therefore, the negative view of growing old persists.

This view among the elderly may have damaging consequences, for it can hardly enhance the quality of one's life to assume that the group with which one is identified is justifiably stereotyped negatively. For younger people, the negative view can only serve to make them fear the future, feel needless pity and guilt over the often exaggerated misery of the old, and to imagine unrealistically that youthful experience is a world apart from that experienced by older people. The negative view directs attention away from the abilities and contributions of the elderly and toward old people as a problem. Younger people may shun the old as harbingers of assumed unhappiness to come, thus both avoiding potentially corrective experiences and avoiding also the pleasure and profit from being with and learning from older people. Such are the prices Americans pay for their value orientation.

There is a third category of ideas that causes distortion of old age in a different way—by romanticizing it. Gubrium provides a convenient summary of the ideas forming the romantic complex:

1. The social environment of old people is conceived as stable and undemanding.
2. The ideal social relationship is portrayed in an image of the 'mutually enriching' elderly couple.
3. Older persons are considered highly altruitic, especially in intergenerational relationships.
4. Aging is a process of diminishing needs and desires.
5. Good health is considered to be an outcome of voluntarily being 'spry' and 'living a healthy life.'
6. Life satisfaction is a general and normal response to aging, being a result of persons adjusting themselves to old age.[23]

Although the romantic complex incorporates positive aspects of old age, they are, as we have suggested earlier, peripheral to the American value system. As in the case of the negative view, the romantic view is found in popular magazines, newspapers, and other news and entertainment media, as well as in retirement brochures. "What is characteristic of such public information on the golden years," notes Gubrium, "is that it is often glib, complacent, and on the whole celebrates old age as a generally peaceful, 'kind,' and happily 'free-of-troubles' period of living. The portrait of elderly persons tends to be one of a collection of 'nice, kind old ladies' that are 'just wonderful people.' "[24] As we can readily see, this positive stereotype stands in marked contrast to surveyed attitudes of the public which are exaggeratedly negative. This contradiction is not without its utility, however, for as Gubrium points out, "The myth [of the Golden Years] allows the devaluation of old age to occur without remorse."[25] His central criticism of this complex of ideas is that it is a set of self-contradictory and often trivial notions that serve as a rationale for conveniently dismissing old age rather than as a basis for challenging the citizenry to demand and carry out remedial social action. If Gubrium's criticisms are correct, we pay another set of prices for social mystification: the frustration of rationally based social policies.

Despite the presence of powerful folk beliefs about old age, studies have emerged which may serve to modify the folk philosophy by revealing what old people themselves report about their own personal experience of being old. These studies can work to reframe our understanding of old age—especially old age as "a problem"—by introducing fresh information and, particularly, different assumptions about the experience of being old in America. This process in turn can give us better understanding of old people's needs and a measure of greater control over meeting them effectively. Reframing, through the incorporation of new assumptions about a problem, can resolve that problem without anything necessarily changing in the objective world. For example, the problems surrounding sexual expressivity among the elderly—often thought abnormal, wrong, and/or repulsive by young *and* old—may be resolved with the adoption of a new assumption (perhaps based on additional information) that old people will normally tend to express themselves sexually when willing and interesting partners are available. Transforming "dirty old men" into "sensuous senior citizens" involves no alteration in the objective sexual biology of elderly homo sapiens, only alteration in the assumptions about the "reality" of that biology.[26] Reframing old age may be seen as part of the knowledge revolution in our time which has placed in new perspectives the life experiences of a number of minority and/or subcultural groups, such as blacks, ethnic groups, and sexual minorities.

The development of new information that leads to reframing phenomena is a cumulative process. This is true of the subject of life satisfaction among the elderly, which evolved as a concern within the broader field of social geronotology.[27] The field of social gerontology emerged in the 1930s because of a new sensitivity to the condition of old people in modernized society. An important research focus was on special social and psychological problems of "adjustment" of old people who were contending with unemployment and income troubles during the Great

Depression. This problem orientation led to an interpretation of aging as a process of decline. The general line of inquiry was about the problems people had in extending their adult kinds of behavior and achievement into old age. The picture that emerged from research in the 1940s and early 1950s ". . . linked positive adjustment to continued activity, social interaction and participation in institutional life, especially work for men and family for women."[28]

Soon, however, social gerontologists shifted their emphasis to a less problem-oriented conceptualization of the aging process. This new orientation underscored "normal" adjustments to changing conditions through the middle and later years. One group of these studies sought to discover if there were discernible trends or variations in the way people played social roles between ages 40 and 70. The results suggested that there were no significant or consistent changes in how people carried out their roles between the ages of 40 and 65, though there were after age 65. Another set of investigations of this age period was centrally concerned with determining if there were age-related changes in the psychology of normal adults. Contradictory conclusions emanated from these investigations, one being that there are no age-related changes in psychological states, and the other being that psychological characteristics do change with age. The studies leading to this second conclusion (reinforced by further researches of "inner" processes) were thought to reveal tendencies among people in their forties and thereafter to turn psychologically inward and away from the "outer world." However, no observable behavioral changes were found in people before age 65 that outwardly revealed the supposed inner psychological processes. A third complex of studies tried to discern "normal" psychological and social changes in people aged 50 to 70—and eventually between 70 and 90. The principal subject of this work was the impact on the individual of the interplay between "outer" performance and "inner" dynamics.

From these groups of studies, several findings were combined to formulate the beginnings of a major theory of life satisfaction. Changes in the social roles of people around 65 years of age (such as retirement, loss of spouse, etc.) were associated with turning inward psychologically, and the basic ideas of disengagement theory emerged:

The interiorization of ego was viewed as an intrinsic developmental process tied to biological change whose effects became apparent in overt behavior during the mid-60's. This interiorization was seen as a psychological disengagement followed by later social disengagement. The latter process was viewed as normal, natural and welcomed by the aging individual as a means of restoring an equilibrium between inner and outer events that had been disturbed by the decline in ego energy and resultant effectiveness of ego functions . . . Additionally, the older person should exhibit a higher subjective sense of well-being, conceptualized as morale, before and after the process of social disengagement than during it since he would be moving into a new, though qualitatively different, equilibrium between himself and society replacing the one that had existed in the middle years.[29]

Disengagement theory has dominated gerontologists' understanding of life satisfaction, but the theory has not gone unchallenged;[30] nor is it without important theoretical competitors. Each major theory can be viewed as a reframing of old age. That is, each theory builds systematically on certain assumptions and observations in order to make sense out of the aging process. People's responses to theories of old age are likely to be emotional as well as thoughtful. Therefore, perceiving the later years as a period of mutual withdrawal between self and society is likely to trigger one set of emotional responses to the prospect of growing old or to the appropriate ways of relating to older people. On the other hand, a perception of old age that involves the older person's continued striving to prolong behavior patterns of middle age is likely to elicit in us an entirely different set of emotional responses.

One major competitor of disengagement theory is activity theory,[31] which states that people will try to continue living according to the patterns of their middle years as long as possible, despite chronological aging. There has been far less scholarly treatment of this than of disengagement theory, although activity theory is a common guide to action programs for the elderly.[32] The assumptions basic to this way of framing old age are conveyed by the compliment, "You're remarkable: you never seem to grow old!" This remark implies that the old person recognizes the continuing imperatives of the norms of middle age and succeeds in living by them. The compliment also assumes that it is right and proper to judge people by the standards of middle age—that an old person should make every effort to remain middle aged. He will not want to give up habitual roles, as disengagement theory would argue, but he will strive to continue playing middle-age roles, or playing useful new roles if previous ones must be dropped. Life satisfaction will be high for a person who maintains his roles rather than reducing them, as disengagement theory would have it.

Activity theory applies well to those who are physically healthy and vigorous, which is, of course, an ever larger subgroup in our modern society. But for the many people in later life for whom aging has brought significant physical deterioration, the theory applies less well. Activity theory can help to keep us from assuming that a person's accumulation of years is, in itself, equivalent to his feeling and/or acting "old."

The contrasts in framing old age according to disengagement and activity theories are succinctly stated by Atchley:

> The activity theory could . . . be expected to apply quite accurately to the chronologically old but still healthy and energetic person. In terms of disengagement theory, this person would not yet be ready for disengagement. This would mean, for example, that when society forces a man not yet ready for disengagement to retire, he might fit the activity theory of aging by attempting to replace the lost role. The theory of societal disengagement would explain why he might be unsuccessful, but the activity theory would explain why he would keep trying.[33]

While the two theories regard old age differently, they hold some assumptions in common. As Orbach points out, disengagement and activity theory share a developmental perspective. In this perspective there are normal processes of aging, and these processes serve society's needs. For both theories:

> Normal aging is cast in a developmental framework which involes the priority of biological, physiological and inner psychic development over the socially learned patterns of role behavior. External manifestations of the psychology and social psychology of the individual, personality, and the subjective sense of well-being, are all reactive responses and adjustments to the inner processes against the setting of the challenges to functional adaptations posed by the external environment.[34]

A third major framing of old age, which has just begun to be researched, is continuity theory. Unlike disengagement and activity theory, continuity theory is not developmental: that is, it poses no states of normal or normative growth, nor any necessary end-states required by society. The principle assumption of continuity theory is that a person wishes to maintain throughout life familiar and habitual patterns of living; however, a person can be flexible in modifying these patterns in response to the multiplicity of special combinations of psychological, biological, and social factors that occur in his life. Thus, while a person will want, for example, to eat, sleep, work, and play as he has before, he may change the way he goes about these activities. He may choose to replace lost or relinquished roles, or he may not. High morale, then, will be the result of successful adaptation to new contingencies. The distinguishing assumption in continuity theory is that a person may adapt in *any* direction, whereas the previously discussed theories presuppose one-directional development in later life. The drawback of continuity theory is that it assumes enormously varied and complex experience among the elderly. Since the theory encompasses so much, it is difficult to utilize as a basis for variable selection, concept definition, or prediction, even though it may best represent what happens to people as they grow old.

The appeal of continuity theory is that it attributes to a person a never-ending capacity to change—either by reorganizing his life according to familiar assumptions, or, more dramatically, according to newly adopted assumptions which alter his perception of "reality." However, a theory's appeal is no measure of its worth, and the validity of continuity theory is largely unresearched at present.

From this brief overview of theories in social gerontology, one can recognize a groping for theoretical adequacy similar to that often found in other social scientific fields. There is no one theoretical perspective at present that preeminently commands the allegience of people working in the field of social gerontology. As Atchley observes,

> . . . none of the existing theories can completely explain aging in modern society. The responsible investigator must constantly compare the situation he is attempting to explain with the existing theories and be ready to invent a new explanation if none of the ready-made ones works.[35]

Our work reflects the problematic search for a theoretical lense through which to view the "reality" of old age. When we began our study of the urban elderly, we held no strong commitment to any one theory, which we believe was appropriate given the fluid state of theory in social gerontology. However, as we examined the data—collected from elderly people themselves as they reported their experiences of old age—it became increasingly clear that a new integrative theoretical approach is most appropriate. We come to this point of view by taking an holistic approach to life satisfaction of the elderly. That is, we attempt to show how a multiplicity of factors actually work upon one another to affect life satisfaction. We find some surprises in that not all the factors generally thought to impact on life satisfaction do so; while other factors (or combinations of them) influence life satisfaction in unanticipated ways. We believe that an holistic approach is particularly well-suited to comprehending the complex forces working on old people as they go about living on the cutting edge of fresh daily experience.

Notes

1. Robert J. Havighurst and Ruth Albrecht, *Older People* (New York: Longmans, Green & Co., 1953), p. 48.

2. Clark Tibbitts, ed., *Handbook of Social Gerontology* (Chicago: The University of Chicago Press, 1960), pp. 292–94.

3. Havighurst and Albrecht, *op. cit.*, Chapter 17.

4. Bernard Kutner, *et al., Five Hundred Over Sixty: A Community Survey on Aging* (New York: Russell Sage Foundation, 1956), pp. 302–3.

5. Leo Srole, "Social Integration and Certain Corollaries: An Exploratory Study," *American Sociological Review*, vol. 21 (1956), pp. 709–16, especially 712–13.

6. Marjorie Fiske Lowenthal, Majda Thurnher, David Chiriboga and Associates, *Four Stages of Life* (San Francisco: Jossey-Bass Publishers, 1975), p. 86.

7. Gordon F. Streib, "Intergenerational Relations: Perspectives of the Two Generations on the Older Parent," *Journal of Marriage and the Family*, vol. 27 (November, 1965), 469–76.

8. Robert J. Berkhofter, *A Behavioral Approach to Historical Analysis* (New York: The Free Press, 1969). See regarding the "truth" and "falseness" of myths, pp. 122-25.

9. Louis Harris and Associates, Inc., *The Myth and Reality of Aging in America* (Washington, D.C.: National Council on Aging, Inc., 1975), p. 129.

10. Jaber F. Gubrium, *The Myth of the Golden Years* (Springfield, Ill.: Charles C. Thomas, 1973), p. 204.

11. Edward T. Hall, *The Silent Language* (New York: Doubleday, 1973), p. 89.

12. Gubrium, *op. cit.*, pp. 204-5.

13. Harris, *op. cit.*, p. 129.

14. Gordon and Walter Moss, *Growing Old* (New York: Pocket Books, 1975), pp. 17-18.

15. Harris, *op. cit.*, p. 142.

16. *Ibid.*, p. 30.

17. *Ibid.*

18. *Ibid.*

19. *Ibid.*

20. *Ibid.*, p. 142.

21. Seymour J. Mandelbaum, *Community and Communications* (New York: W. Norton & Co., Inc., 1972), p. 19.

22. Harris, *op. cit.*, p. 38. See also p. 35. Rosenfelt calls the negative self-image of the elderly, "the elderly mystique," the etiology of which she accounts for as follows:

> The elderly mystique got underway at the same time and took form as the psychosocial reflection of rapidly accelerated conditions of technological development, sequelae of the prolonged period of global war. Obsolescent skills of the aging, overcrowding of the ranks of labor, and the growth of social security and retirement plans profoundly changed the anticipations of those entering the aged cohorts. With the changed anticipations, many of a negative sort, there developed new attitudes toward old age itself. In short, (although this oversimplified statement does violence to the complexities of the situation) the elderly mystique resulted from major technological and social changes associated with World War II and evolved and crystalized into a complex of feelings shared by many of today's old people.

Rosalie H. Rosenfelt, "The Elderly Mystique," *Journal of Social Issues*, vol. 21 (1965), pp. 37-43, see p. 38.

23. Gubrium, *op. cit.*, p. 200.

24. *Ibid.*, p. 184.

25. *Ibid.*

26. Paul Watzlawick, *et al.*, *Change: Principles of Problem Formation and Problem Resolution* (New York: W. W. Norton, 1973).

27. The next several paragraphs draw heavily on Harold L. Orbach, "The

Disengagement Theory of Aging, 1960–1970: A Case Study of Scientific Controversy" (Ph. D. Dissertation, University of Minnesota, 1974), pp. 70–76. See also "The Disengagement Controversy," forthcoming in *Human Development,* 1977.

28. *Ibid.,* p. 71.

29. *Ibid.,* pp. 74–75.

30. For criticisms of disengagement theory, see Chapter 2 of this book. See also Orbach, pp. 92–117, and Robert C. Atchley, *The Social Forces in Later Life: An Introduction to Social Gerontology* (Belmont, Cal.: Wadsworth, 1972), pp. 33–34.

31. In this review of theories, we draw especially on Atchley, *ibid.,* pp. 31-39.

32. Atchley, *ibid.,* p. 34.

33. *Ibid.,* p. 35.

34. *Ibid.,* p. 101.

35. *Ibid.,* p. 39.

TWO

The Official View: Studies of Life Satisfaction

Introduction

Older people share with other age groups the necessity of operating within given social and economic environments. For the most part, such environments are not created with the needs of older people in mind. Still, the way a particular environment is structured will influence the older person's perception of himself and others and will, to some extent, determine the scope and direction of his activities. If an environment, by design or chance, includes convenient transportation, safe neighborhoods, adequate health care facilities, and the like, the older person's life experiences are likely to be more satisfying. On the other hand, an environment that lacks such attributes decidedly limits a person's chances of achieving a satisfying life in his later years. Thus, the environment confronting the older person may represent either opportunity or obstacle.

A scholar interested in studying the determinants of life satisfaction must take into account the interrelation between the structure of the environment and the personal characteristics of people in that environment. At times this interrelation can become quite complex. For example, the extent of an elderly person's present participation in social organizations may be influenced by attitudes internalized earlier in life, but which may be modified by the current proximity in the environment of both other people his own age and meeting places for such organizations. The plethora of factors, both personal and environmental, creates a problem of selectivity for the investigator. Even when this problem is solved to his own satisfaction, he must further decide on appropriate methods of comparing or relating the phenomena he has selected. In general, he will want to deal with a large enough set of factors to provide a relatively comprehensive picture of the determinants of life satisfaction, while at the same time using procedures that integrate the varied phenomena so that the people being studied do not become mere abstractions.

With this in mind, we will devote the balance of the chapter to an examination of representative and/or seminal works in the literature of life satisfaction among the elderly. Our primary objective in this review is to identify the determinants of life satisfaction that emerge from the studies. In subsequent chapters we will attempt to define the interrelationships among these determinants by including them in an analysis of a sample of elderly urban residents.

The Constituents of Life Satisfaction

The social gerontologist's concern for individual well-being is indicated by the central position that the subject of life satisfaction occupies in research on the social aspects of aging. At the same time, studies of life satisfaction reflect a variety of research objectives and approaches, and it is difficult to draw confident generalizations from this body of literature. Generalizations that order the determinants of life satisfaction and express relationships among them have yet to be fully developed in this field of investigation. Yet, researchers attempting to make such generalizations must build upon the observations and insights contained in the existing literature; and the studies to be reviewed do provide fundamental insights into the factors most likely to impact directly on the life satisfaction of elderly people.

Through researchers' procedures, we are able to identify two general types of life satisfaction studies: "comparative" and "correlate." Some authors compare samples drawn from populations embodying special characteristics, thereby controlling for assumed intervening factors. For example, an investigator might assume that a person's physical health is an intervening variable in the determination of life satisfaction. He might, therefore, compare a sample of older people who had been hospitalized in the past year with a sample of older people who had not been hospitalized. A similar example is to examine the effects of living in age-integrated communities versus the effects of living in age-segregated (retirement) communities. In correlate studies, authors have focused on life satisfaction as the one dependent variable and on selected independent variables as potential correlates of life satisfaction, the relationships being tested within an undifferentiated sample. For example, an investigator might test the extent to which socioeconomic status and physical health are correlated with the level of a person's life satisfaction. We do not mean to imply that, within these two broad categories, life satisfaction studies are completely uniform. However, this procedural distinction appears to have some effect on the respective findings of the two types of studies.

Perhaps the most provocative work in the field of social gerontology is that of Cumming and Henry. Theirs was one of the first efforts to build a social theory of aging, which they termed "disengagement." The theory of disengagement was undoubtedly the most notable outgrowth of the three Kansas City Studies of the 1950s, conducted under the auspices of the University of Chicago's Committee on Human Development. The theory was comprehensive, said to apply universally, and offered a predictive model. As such, it provided a persuasive and coherent framework in which much subsequent research was to be conducted. Orbach has carefully described the manner in which disengagement theory emerged from the work of several research teams, each team using different methoifferent objectives. This research led to "different results obtained from separate analyses performed upon the same basic set of interview data utilizing selected parts of the information collected."[1] The character of these results does not produce an appropriate baseline for comparison over time with our findings. Nevertheless, the disengagement perspective remains relevant to our inquiry.

Essentially, disengagement refers to a process whereby society and an aged individual, in preparation for the individual's impending death, mutually withdraw from each other. Cumming and Henry contended that this process is functionally necessary as well as universal. In the years since its publication, their work has been both widely used and widely criticized. A large share of the criticism has revolved around the assumption of functional necessity implicit in disengagement theory. For instance, Rose, among other criticisms, objects to the proposition that disengagement is necessary for satisfactory adjustment to old age. Citing evidence gathered by Havighurst and his associates, Rose concludes that, "The engaged elderly, rather than the disengaged, are the ones who generally, although not always, are happiest and have the greatest expressed life satisfaction."[2]

Cumming and Henry studied a sample of Kansas City, Missouri residents 50 years of age and older. Although the subjects were relatively homogeneous (i.e., all were physically healthy adults without pressing economic worries), Cumming and Henry divided them into four groups representing categories corresponding to their concept of disengagement. Group One was "fully engaged," Group Four was "fully disengaged," and the other two groups represented intermediate stages. Members of the fully engaged group were married women and working men under 65 years of age who had high perceived "life space." Members of the fully disengaged group were men and women over 65, not married and not working, who had low perceived "life space." Life satisfaction is represented by the subject's level of morale, which the authors attempted to measure with the Srole and Kutner scales. However, they found these scales unreliable for their sample and finally "resorted to a direct and intuitive judgment of the level of the respondent's morale."[3] They found the highest levels of morale at the beginning (Group One) and end (Group Four) stages of the disengagement process, and the lowest morale at the intermediate stages.

In light of these findings, Cumming and Henry suggest that morale varies with disengagement. But do the findings necessarily support this contention? Since age itself was a major criterion in forming the disengagement categories, in the analysis age acts as an intervening influence on the relationship between disengagement and morale. Thus, either age (and all that may entail) or disengagement may account for the variation in morale. To eliminate this ambiguity, it would be necessary to establish: the relationship between disengagement and morale while holding age constant; and the relationship between age and morale while holding disengagement constant. Moreover, it is possible that people in Group One occupied social roles among which there was essential accord. The people constituting Group Four may have had a similar consonance in their lives, while people in the intermediate groups were experiencing disruptions in their social roles. It may have been the relative consonance that accounted for the variation in morale in the Cumming and Henry study. While the disruptions older people experience can be special to their age-group (such as retirement), the general phenomenon could occur at most age levels. Whether this is the case or not, the concept of disengagement will become part of our analysis through its constituent parts—age, sex, employment, and marital status.

The influence of age integration and age segregation on life satisfaction is analyzed by Poorkaj. He studies three random matched samples: one exclusively from the Pasadena Senior Center (California) representing "engaged" older adults belonging to social organizations; a second comprised of beneficiaries of five health and welfare agencies in Pasadena, "disengaged" from active group participation; and a third who were residents of an activity-oriented, age-segregated housing community. Poorkaj measures life satisfaction by selecting 13 items from morale scales developed by Havighurst, Kutner, Srole, and Cumming and Henry. He interprets his findings as supporting disengagement theory to some degree, "in that a disengagement within an integrated community does not necessarily manifest itself in a lower level of morale for the aged."[4] But he sees as his most significant finding the fact that those living in the age-integrated community had higher morale than those living in the age-segregated retirement community. Thus, we add the concept of age-integration to that of disengagement for inclusion in our analysis.

In his study of family status and extra-familial age-groupings among the elderly, Messer examines the effect of age concentration in housing environments on the morale of older people. His data were derived from a probability sample of residents of two types of housing units in Chicago. One sample is taken from tenants of public housing projects occupied exclusively by people over 62 years of age. The other sample is derived from people over 62 years of age residing in public housing projects of mixed-age composition. Using the morale scale developed by Kutner, Messer finds that those living in an age-concentrated housing environment had higher morale than those living in mixed-age housing environments. He reports that "This tendency was maintained when race, age, sex, and health status were added to the analysis as control variables."[5] Differences in income level between the two sample groups are controlled for implicitly since eligibility for public housing presupposes a relatively low income. Thus, Messer's findings, in his study of different housing environments, are at variance with those of Poorkaj in his study of different community environments.

While the housing environment is not a focus of this study, Messer's analysis bears upon our own in that he suggests the concept "age concentration." This term is actually more descriptive of age compositions found in the community environments represented in our study than other terms such as "age integration" or "age homogeneity." So, in the text, we will often use the term "age concentration" in our discussions, although the more frequently-used term "age integration" appears in our graphic models.

Gubrium highlights the importance of social context to the aged in his theoretical examination of a socio-environmental approach to aging. He draws on previous studies indicating that the meaning for old people of such occurrences as widowhood, retirement, and poverty depend on the social context in which they happen. One particular empirical source to which he refers is the Detroit Study, which in general tends to corroborate the previous socio-environmental studies.[6] The Detroit Study is based on a sample of 210 people, age 60 to 94, that was drawn for observation and interview from three types of social contexts differing in degree of age concentration.

Regarding morale, Gubrium argues that "variations in the burdens of social contexts are significant in their impact on the morale of persons."[7] In age-heterogeneous situations (which include a mix of old and young people), an old person will probably face a maximum variety of social situations, and a commensurate variety of activities and intensities of activity will be expected of him by people of various ages. An old person's ease in performing one activity may not mean similar ease in other activities. For the older person, such a spectrum of activities and expectations can be burdensome. In an age-homogeneous context (composed entirely of older people), on the other hand, the sorts of social situations and expectations are comparatively few, and an old person's ability to meet demands easily in one social situation means he probably can meet other situations with similar ease. It would follow from Gubrium's argument that morale tends to be higher in age-homogeneous social contexts, which contradicts the major conclusion of Poorkaj outlined above.

From another aspect of the socio-environmental perspective, Gubrium finds that morale is affected by congruence between an older person's individual context and his social context. That is, a person sees himself as having a certain pattern of activity resources for behaving which give him a degree of flexibility, on the basis of which he expects to be able to meet daily problems. A person also knows that relevant other people around him have in mind certain expectations about behavior which influence him. Thus, from the individual's point of view, he expects certain behaviors from himself (individual context) and he knows others expect certain behaviors from him (social context). Gubrium argues that an old person's satisfaction with self and his living conditions will be highest when there is congruence between what he expects of himself and what significant others expect of him; and satisfaction will be lowest when there is incongruence between these dual expectations.[8]

Gubrium's conclusion adds weight to our suggestion (see p. 00) that role consonance/dissonance, rather than engagement/disengagement, may have been responsible for the variations in morale reported by Cumming and Henry. Clearly, his discussion of socio-environmental factors relating to life satisfaction underscores the relevance of age-integration to our analysis.

Kutner and his associates studied the responses of a sample of people over 60 from the Kips Bay–Yorkville area of New York City. They constructed a morale scale which indicated the presence or absence of satisfaction, optimism, and "an expanding life perspective." Respondents were divided into nearly equal groups of high, medium and low morale scores. Kutner's most general conclusion is that morale declines gradually and systematically with increasing age. However, he did find some differences between the sexes. The morale of women declines gradually while that of men declines relatively sharply between 65 and 69 and experiences a mild upturn between the ages of 70 and 74. These findings are somewhat at variance with those of Cumming and Henry, who found little change in the morale of female respondents throughout the four disengagement stages.[9] The precipitous decline of morale in men found by Kutner is probably due to the impact of retirement which, in most cases, does not affect women as directly.

In addition to age, Kutner finds the following factors to be associated with variations in morale: socioeconomic status; poor health in low status respondents only; marital status (with married persons having higher morale than single persons, and widows occupying an intermediate position); and employment. Socioeconomic status and physical health will be added to the list of factors in our analysis; marital status, age, and employment are, of course, already part of that list.

Kutner also concludes that working is a more important factor than the level of income. He also studied the influences of activity and social isolation on the morale of his subjects and concludes that his findings offer only partial and highly qualified support for the notion that "the busy older person is the happy individual."[10] Activity to fill free time, he suggests, is less likely to produce good adjustment than is gainful activity. Activity will be included in our analysis, but as part of the concept of social participation.

Cutler studied a sample of non-institutionalized persons 65 and older from Oberlin, Ohio. He was primarily concerned with the effect of voluntary association participation on life satisfaction, but he also included in his analysis two other independent variables, socioeconomic status and self-rated health. He found a positive relation between the extent of voluntary association participation and life satisfaction. Both socioeconomic status and self-rated health also were found to be significantly related to life satisfaction, but after controlling for these two variables, the relation between voluntary association participation and life satisfaction was reduced to a level below statistical significance.[11] From this Cutler concludes that "voluntary associations self-select as members and as participants persons who are initially more satisfied with their life situation because of their health and status characteristics." Cutler, as he himself points out, deals only with an aggregated set of many types of voluntary associations, and he recognizes the possibility that participation in certain types of organizations might have impacts on the personal adjustments of the aged.[12] The concept of social participation, then, is added to our analysis.

Edwards and Klemmack examined the effect of a wide range of variables on life satisfaction. The data used in their study were obtained from a sample of middle-aged and elderly persons residing in a Virginia four-county area. The subjects were predominantly white, Anglo-Saxon Protestants. Twenty-two independent variables were used in a multiple regression analysis.[13] Results of the analysis indicate that the primary determinants of life satisfaction are: socioeconomic status, particularly family income; and non-familial participation, particularly neighboring. According to their findings, perceived health is also related to life satisfaction while the number of experienced ailments is not. They further suggest that activity in general does not contribute to life satisfaction, but only particular types of activity. That is, formal participation is not found to be related to life satisfaction while informal participation is. Finally, the relationship between age and life satisfaction, they find, is reduced to a level below statistical significance when socio-economic status is held constant.

From their findings, Edwards and Klemmack construct a hypothetical causal model in which socioeconomic status impacts directly on life satisfaction and indirectly through perceived health and informal participation.[14] These three variables, as they are related to each other in the above model, will be included in our analysis (with "informal participation" being part of "social participation"). The hypothetical model could have been tested by Edwards and Klemmack if the intervening variables, health and participation, had also been treated as dependent variables.

Drawing on data collected by the National Opinion Research Center at the University of Chicago, Spreitzer and Snyder investigate the correlates of life satisfaction among older people. The use of this data provided them with the advantage of a national probability sample but left them with the disadvantage of relatively gross measures of their key variables. Life satisfaction, health, financial status, and social class were all determined by self-ratings, which in itself is a valid procedure. However, each measure was determined by the response to a single question, such as "If you were asked to use one of four names for your social class, which would you say you belong in: the lower class, the working class, the middle class, or the upper class?"[15]

To an extent, the Spreitzer and Snyder findings concur with those of Edwards and Klemmack, in that perceived health condition and financial status are found to be predictors of life satisfaction. However, they add one qualification: "Perceived financial adequacy was a substantially stronger predictor of life satisfaction than were . . . objective indicators of socioeconomic position."[16] This qualification will be taken into account in our analysis. On the other hand, their findings appear to be contradictory to some we have previously encountered in regard to the relationship among age, sex and life satisfaction. They find that up to age 65 women tend to report higher rates of life satisfaction than men; whereas after 65, men are more predisposed than women to indicate a high degree of life satisfaction.

Cameron uses samples from three distinct elderly populations to study "ego strength" and happiness. The populations are: people maintaining their own homes; people residing in a cooperative "golden years" complex; and hospitalized people (the type of hospital is not specified). He also compares the total elderly sample—over 59—with a control group of younger people—18 to 40. He finds that "ego strength" is lower among the elderly group than the younger group, while the proportion of "happy moods" as contrasted to "sad moods" is not significantly different between the two groups. However, among the three elderly subsamples, he finds significant differences in "ego strength." Those who maintain their own homes have the highest "ego strength." "Those who have surrendered some degree of their independence to cooperative living . . . "[17] occupy an intermediate position. The hospitalized, who are the most dependent, exhibit the lowest "ego strength." Thus, the concept of independence is added to the list of variables in our analysis.

Cameron equates ego strength with morale which in turn is defined as "felt competency." Therefore, his findings appear to be somewhat tautological for, in effect, he is concluding that as people become less capable of managing their own lives, they experience a corresponding decline in felt competency. However, Cameron's analysis bears on our own in that it calls attention to the definition of morale. The relationship between personal competency and morale is certainly worth investigating, but rather than equating the two concepts we believe a distinction should be made between them. A preferred conception of morale would indicate feelings of well-being and satisfaction with life in general, which actually comes closer to Cameron's "happiness" than to felt competency, although morale should denote more than simply happy moods.

From a sample of people in the San Francisco area, Clark and Anderson examine, among other things, the morale of elderly people. Their principal objective was to examine stress among the aged, and since being placed in the category "mentally ill" is inherently stressful, they control for mental illness by separating their sample into three groups based on psychiatric histories.[18] They conducted intensive interviews with a subsample of respondents. In the analysis of these interviews, they identify the sources of high morale and of dissatisfaction in both "community" subjects and hospitalized subjects. We will consider the findings pertaining to the community subjects only since they are most relevant to our study. According to these findings, sources of high morale are, in descending order: entertainments and diversions, socializing, physical comforts, and financial security.[19] We conclude our list of concepts to be associated with life satisfaction by adding entertainments and physical security. Socializing already has been accounted for by "social participation," and in our analysis physical comforts is subsumed under physical security.

The index of morale that Clark and Anderson use in their study is consistent with what we believe to be the preferred conceptualization of the term. They describe their scale as "a bi-polar dimension indicating depression at the one pole and satisfaction at the other."[20] The items of their scale elicit responses indicating a person's feelings about his general condition and about his attitudes toward life in general. With some modification, which will be discussed in the next chapter, we use the Clark and Anderson morale scale as the central measure of life satisfaction in our analysis.[21]

The studies we have reviewed, considered together, provide a comprehensive picture of the wide range of experiences in old age that affect life satisfaction. Though the picture is comprehensive, it is not always consistent. One interesting difference between the comparative and correlate studies is that the former do not attribute special significance to socioeconomic status while the latter consistently ascribe importance to it as an influence on morale. The comparative studies, as we have mentioned, are concerned with special properties of sample groups, e.g., age-segregated versus age-integrated living arrangements. Therefore, when comparative samples are more-or-less socioeconomically homogeneous, socioeconomic status is implicitly held constant but its impact on life satisfaction is not explicitly tested. When, on the other hand, comparative samples are not socioeconomically homogeneous, this characteristic tends to be ignored. Furthermore, because of this emphasis on special groups, the findings of comparative studies tend not to cohere, and it is therefore difficult to establish an order of relative importance among determinants of life satisfaction. Although the correlate studies are similar to each other in the importance they place on socioeconomic status, in virtually all cases they are testing distinctive variable sets; and while each study tests a variable set on an undifferentiated sample, the populations from which the samples are drawn tend to vary from one study to another, in regard to demographic characteristics. For these reasons, the results of the correlate studies also are not generally cumulative.

Our critique of important studies concerned with life satisfaction in old age illustrates some of the research problems encountered in an area of investigation that has had a relatively short history. Similar problems were observed in the early studies of the psychological motivations for fertility behavior. In 1954, Borgatta and Westoff acknowledged certain methodological problems in responding to criticism of such studies.

> The criticism that the data have been approached atomistically derives from two arguments—that the individuals and couples who were interviewed were treated more as a series of traits, characteristics, and attitudes than as whole people, and secondly that the data were analyzed hypothesis by hypothesis with little attempt at integration. The first criticism is valid and perhaps somewhat characteristic of

statistical studies in this area in general; the latter objection has been met in part by the Westoff and Kiser article and in part by this work.[22]

But four years later, in their summary report of the Indianapolis Study, Kiser and Whelpton perceptively observed that problems of atomism do not easily disappear.

> In a very real way [the separate analysis of the variable under each hypothesis] necessitates the assumption that all other factors are equal when groups are classified on the basis of only one variable at a time. The atomistic approach neglects the sociological and psychological axiom that motivations are multiple and complex. It is true that some attempt has been made to investigate the simultaneous impact of several variables . . . but the Study was structured and the results were analyzed largely in terms of twenty-three separate hypotheses.[23]

Thus at some point it is necessary to go beyond separate hypothesis-testing and to achieve some means of integrating the findings pertaining to the subject at hand. We will attempt to take this additional step by creating a causal-analytic framework within which to examine life satisfaction.

Clemente and Sauer raise the question of whether or not the study of life satisfaction is sufficiently advanced to make causal modeling beneficial. In explaining why they do not attempt such a procedure, they suggest that methodologies employed in life satisfaction studies are too rudimentary to support convincing generalizations. They also cite Campbell, who is in agreement with our central criticism that the study of life satisfaction has been uncoordinated and that, for the most part, results in this area have not been cumulative. Clemente and Sauer therefore conclude, "From this perspective it can be strongly argued that the testing of explicit hypotheses constitutes a necessary first step in setting the stage for the development of more complex causal models."[24]

We agree that problems still exist in the study of life satisfaction. But in the field of social gerontology at least, the "first step" in the study of life satisfaction has been underway for more than a decade. Whereas hypothesis testing is always an important part of research design, more testing of isolated hypotheses will produce more of what critics have found objectionable in life satisfaction research to date. In light of the studies just reviewed, it is our contention that a sufficient basis for examining patterns of relationships leading to life satisfaction exists in the field at the present time. The authors of life satisfaction studies, though vulnerable to the criticisms outlined here and by others, have provided a number of insights regarding the determinants of life satisfaction and these, along with the logic of temporal relations among variables,[25] should enable investigators to model causal networks and to test their models. We also feel that it is only by examining each variable in the context of such a network that its contribution to life satisfaction can be sufficiently understood. This is somewhat analogous to the difference between the occasional chess player, an appellation that would include most of us, and the expert chess player. The occasional player may fully understand the capability of each piece and its relative advantage in achieving the objective of the game. But to play chess well, one must be able to see the ways that the position and function of each piece impinge upon the functioning of many or all other pieces, whether or not they are in positions to immediately threaten the king.

In subsequent chapters we will explore the dynamics of life satisfaction among the urban elderly. We begin this analysis by constructing a theoretical model that integrates virtually all the variables that, according to the studies reviewed here, contribute to life satisfaction. This model is presented in Figure 2.1 Because it takes into account findings of all the studies, it may not represent exactly the findings of any one study.

Two clusters of factors affecting life satisfaction are apparent in the model. The four variables at the top of the figure actually constitute the concept of disengagement as formulated by Cumming and Henry. This concept has figured prominently in social gerontological thought and is particularly evident in the comparative type studies. The second cluster includes variables theoretically connected to the concept of socioeconomic status, which assumes such an important role in the correlate studies. The three remaining variables (at the bottom of the figure) represent three more-or-less discrete influences on life satisfaction, according to the literature. The overall configuration of the model portrays spatially two distinct categories of variables. Those variables constituting the inner circle (i.e., those closest to life

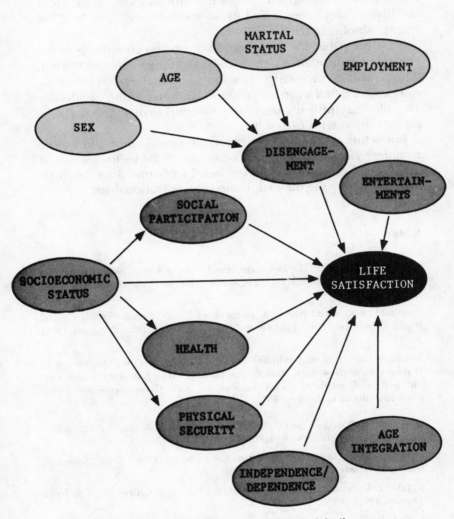

Figure 2.1 A Theoretical Model of Life Satisfaction

satisfaction) represent relatively contemporary phenomena that are more subject to change than the variables constituting the outer circle. These latter variables represent relatively fixed conditions in the lives of older people and in the case of "age" and "sex," of course, absolutely fixed conditions.

One thing that the model does not express completely is the interrelationships among the variables leading to life satisfaction. Thus it will be necessary to develop additional models before we can explore the effect on life satisfaction of intervening variables or variables that influence life satisfaction only to the extent that they act in concert with each other.

But before we can test the theoretical model and explore more complex relationships, it will be necessary for us to describe in some detail our research procedures. In Chapter 3 we begin by describing how the theoretical model is operationalized.

Notes

1. Harold L. Orbach, "The Disengagement Theory of Aging, 1960–1970: A Case Study of Scientific Controversy" (Ph. D. Dissertation, University of Minnesota, 1974), p. 80.

2. Arnold M. Rose and Warren A. Peterson, eds., *Older People and Their Social World: The Sub-Culture of the Aging* (Philadelphia: F. A. Davis Company, 1965), p. 363.

3. Elaine Cumming and William E. Henry, *Growing Old: The Process of Disengagement* (New York: Basic Books, 1961), p. 131. It is doubtful whether the "fully engaged" group should be considered elderly since it includes people in their fifties and only up to the age of 65.

4. Houshang Poorkaj, "Social-Psychological Factors and 'Successful Again,' " *Sociology and Social Research* (April, 1972), p. 299.

5. Mark Messer, "Age Grouping and the Family Status of the Elderly," *Sociology and Social Research*, vol. 52 (1968), p. 275.

6. Jaber F. Gubrium, *The Myth of the Golden Years* (Springfield, Ill.: Charles C. Thomas, 1973), p. 59.

7. *Ibid.*, p. 44.

8. *Ibid.* See pp. 59 and 130–31.

9. Like Kutner, Cumming and Henry found that male morale decreased precipitously in the intermediate groups. But in the "fully disengaged" group it

returned to approximately the same level as that of males in the "fully engaged" group, who were all under 65 years of age.

10. Bernard Kutner, *et. al., Five Hundred Over Sixty: A Community Survey on Aging* (New York: Russell Sage Foundation, 1956), p. 121.

11. Stephen J. Cutler, "Voluntary Association Participation and Life Satisfaction: A Cautionary Research Note," *Journal of Gerontology*, vol. 28, no. 1 (1973), p. 99.

12. *Ibid.*

13. John N. Edwards and David L. Klemmack, "Correlates of Life Satisfaction: A Re-examination," *Journal of Gerontology*, vol. 28, no. 4 (1973), 497–502.

14. Together these three variables explain most of the variance in life satisfaction in the Edwards and Klemmack sample.

15. Elmer Spreitzer and Eldon E. Snyder, "Correlates of Life Satisfaction Among the Aged," *Journal of Gerontology*, vol. 29, no. 4 (1974), 454–58.

16. *Ibid.*, p. 455.

17. Paul Cameron, "Ego Strength and Happiness of the Aged," *Journal of Gerontology*, vol. 22, no. 2 (April 1967), 201-2.

18. The three groups are: 264 "community" subjects with no psychiatric hospitalization; 90 discharged hospital subjects with no psychiatric hospitalization before age 60; and 81 hospitalized patients with no psychiatric hospitalization before age 60.

19. Margaret Clark and Barbara G. Anderson, *Culture and Aging* (Springfield, Ill.: Charles C. Thomas, 1967), p. 219.

20. *Ibid.*, p. 449.

21. For a discussion of various life satisfaction measures and the correlations among them, see Nancy Lohmann, "Correlations of Life Satisfaction, Morale and Adjustment Measures," *Journal of Gerontology*, vol. 32, no. 1 (1977), pp. 73–75.

22. Edgar F. Borgatta and Charles F. Westoff, "The Prediction of Total Fertility," *Milbank Memorial Fund Quarterly* (XXV), vol. 32, no. 4 (October, 1954), pp. 385–86.

23. Clyde Kiser and Pascal K. Whelpton, "Summary of Chief Findings and Implications for Future Studies," *Milbank Memorial Fund Quarterly (XXXIII)*, vol. 36, no. 3 (July, 1958), p. 323.

24. Frank Clemente and William J. Sauer, "Life Satisfaction in the United States," *Social Forces*, vol. 54, no. 3 (March, 1976), p. 625.

25. For our sample of elderly people (for example), certain aspects of life belong to the past. For instance, we would judge formal education to be an independent variable since it is unlikely that the extent of one's formal schooling will be influenced by current events.

THREE

Concepts and Real People: A Methodology

Introduction

All of the models developed in the present study are rather precisely and logically defined analogs of the ways in which people experience old age. The model presented at the end of Chapter 2 expresses relationships that are expectations based on knowledge acquired from a body of relevant literature. This chapter describes the procedures through which we attempt to reach two objectives: the first is to operationalize the theoretical model (Fig. 2.1) by substituting empirical indicators for the concepts contained in the model; the second is to test the model in the broadest possible context of other potential determinants of life satisfaction.

According to Dubin, a researcher may take one of two approaches to any theoretical model: he may seek to prove the adequacy of that model; or he may seek to improve upon it. If one seeks proof of the adequacy of a model, the primary task is to establish some reasonable criteria for "rejecting experimental results that do not conform to the hypothetical predictions of his theoretical model." Improvement, on the other hand, requires the researcher to

. . . focus attention particularly on the deviant cases and noncon-
forming results that do not accord with the predictions. . . . From this
standpoint all data that are marshalled in an investigation are likely to

be retained as relevant to the test of the theoretical model. [And also] the intellectually interesting feature of a model is its unexpected outcomes or its disproof, not its proof.[1]

Following Dubin, we do not stress the proof of the model in Figure 2.1, rather we retain all of the statistically significant relationships of the variables within it—as well as those of associated variables— whether they have been predicted or emerge unexpectedly. We take this approach in an effort to improve upon existing models of life satisfaction.

A Testable Model

The objective of the 1974 interview survey, the results of which constitute the data of our study, was to determine for purposes of public policy the needs and major problems of Kansas City's elderly residents. Given the constraints of this objective and the limitations of interview procedures, we developed a set of measures from the interview responses that transform the components of the theoretical model into testable indicators of those components.

The variables that make up the disengagement cluster (AGE, SEX, MARITAL STATUS, EMPLOYMENT) can be measured directly in our data set. The AGE distribution of the people comprising the sample for our interview survey is as follows: 37 percent are between 60 and 69; 44 percent are between 70 and 79; and 19 percent are 80 and older. Fifty-five percent of the sample are female and 45 percent male. Married persons comprised 52 percent of the sample, while 48 percent are not married. Only 16 percent are employed, while 84 percent are not.

For the remaining concepts in the theoretical model, no exact counterparts exist in the data. Therefore, we have constructed indices that stand for the respective concepts, or we have substituted variables that are indicators of the concept but that can be empirically tested. To operationalize socioeconomic status, we use two variables commonly associated with that concept, INCOME and EDUCATION. The income of the sample ranges from $600 to $22,000 per year. The mean income is $4,280 and the distribution is rather widely dispersed (standard deviation = $3,462). EDUCATION is measured in terms of the number of years of formal schooling completed. It should be kept in mind that the formal education of these people took place in the 1920s or earlier. Since expectations concerning an education were not as high then, the educational distribution of the sample is much lower than one would expect for a similar group of people being educated today. Many people have completed no more than an eighth grade education.

The concept of social participation is represented by the variable ACTIVITY. The ACTIVITY index measures the level of a person's participation in a variety of activities, both formal and informal: church attendance; clubs or associations; writing or receiving letters; and hobbies. While hobbies may be pursued individually, they also may be, and often are, a basis for social discourse and interaction.

Health is measured through two variables, MEDICAL and CAPACITY. The MEDICAL index includes a person's report of his past and present experience with medical problems as well as his perception of the current state of his health. CAPACITY involves an individual's ability to perform a graded series of nine everyday household tasks that range from making the bed to shoveling snow (for the complete series of tasks, see Appendix B).

Physical security includes the variable INCOME ADEQUACY and the index CONDITION OF NEIGHBORHOOD. The former refers to whether a respondent's income in the preceding year was not enough to cover expenses, just barely enough to cover expenses, or adequate to cover expenses with money left over. The results of the interview survey indicate that this index measures more than simply the size of one's income. Some people with relatively large incomes indicate that their incomes were just barely adequate and a few even inadequate. Conversely, some respondents with relatively small incomes reported money left over at the end of the year. In addition to income size, then, this measure involves money management and opportunities within given environments to optimize one's income, as well as variations in individual expectations and needs. We assume that an adequate income, regardless of size, contributes to a sense of physical security. The condition of one's neighborhood should also contribute to a sense of physical well-being. CONDITION OF NEIGHBORHOOD refers to a person's evaluation of his neighborhood's safety and attractiveness.

Whether a person is independent or dependent is measured by three variables. The SELF-TRANSPORTATION index measures the extent to which respondents drive themselves to work, the doctor's office, group and church meetings, the drugstore, and the grocery store. In American society, the kind of mobility reflected in the ability to drive oneself is an important indicator of independence. Dependency consists of two indices. DEPENDENCE ON FAMILY gauges the extent to which those interviewed ask the assistance of relatives (other than spouse) in making household repairs, preparing meals, and accomplishing other household chores. Additional items in this index measure the respondents' attitudes about living in the homes of their children and about children caring for older people who can no longer work. Also, respondents were asked if they were visited most often by relatives or by others. The DEPENDENCE ON FRIENDS AND NEIGHBORS index consists of the same types of assistance covered in the previous index.

Age integration is operationalized by the variable PERCENT ELDERLY. This variable actually represents age concentration in that it measures the proportion of people (60 and older) residing in the same census tract as the respondent. It is therefore a somewhat rough measure of the age homogeneity of the older person's immediate environment. In general, the less age homogeneous, the more age integrated the immediate environment would be.

Entertainments are represented in our analysis by the variable MEDIA USE. This index measures the amount of time spent listening to radio and watching television, and the extent to which people read newspapers and magazines.

Finally, the MORALE index, which is discussed in Chapter 2 (p. 31), is an adaptation of the morale scale developed by Clark and Anderson. The complete index is presented in Appendix B. In addition to this relatively objective scale, we constructed another measure of life satisfaction based on unstructured responses to interview questions that were essentially open-ended. From these responses, we determined whether or not: (1) given the opportunity, respondents would change the way they had lived their lives; (2) they judged their lives to be rewarding; (3) life had become worse for them in recent years; (4) they found life particularly difficult; (5) they were satisfied with their immediate environment; and (6) they felt they had any important unmet needs. By scoring each of these questions and combining the scores, we arrived at our PERSONAL SATISFACTION measure.

For both of these measures the numerical mid-point is 4.5. The mean of the PERSONAL SATISFACTION measure for our sample is 5.3 and the standard deviation is 1.7. The mean of the MORALE measure for our sample is 6.06 with a standard deviation of 2.07. If the ranges of the two measures are assumed to represent a true continuum of life satisfaction from its lowest possible point to its highest possible level, then our sample would have above average life satisfaction. While there is a broad range of life satisfaction scores, this relatively high central tendency supports the contention that the negative ideas about old age (discussed in Chapter 1) are exaggerated and thus misleading. At the same time, there are enough people with low life satisfaction to indicate that the "golden years" notion is also an oversimplification. As can be seen, a higher level of life satisfaction is indicated by the MORALE measure with approximately 2/3 of the sample having scores between 4 and 8. By comparison, approximately 2/3 of the sample have PERSONAL SATISFACTION scores between 3.5 and 7. Later in this chapter we will make a more detailed comparison between the two measures, and for reasons to be explained then, MORALE is chosen to represent the concept of life satisfaction in our analysis. The theoretical model of life satisfaction as it is operationalized (with the variables described above) appears in Figure 3.1.

Other Potential Influences on Life Satisfaction

There are, of course, potential influences on life satisfaction beyond those that are identified by life satisfaction studies as being particularly important. Moreover, we feel that an explanation of life satisfaction is best served by incorporating in a single analysis as many potential relationships as possible. Therefore, in addition to the variables appearing in the operationalized model, our analysis incorporates a set of variables that logically could be classified as either (1) direct influences on life satisfaction that have not been identifed previously, or (2) part of that network of

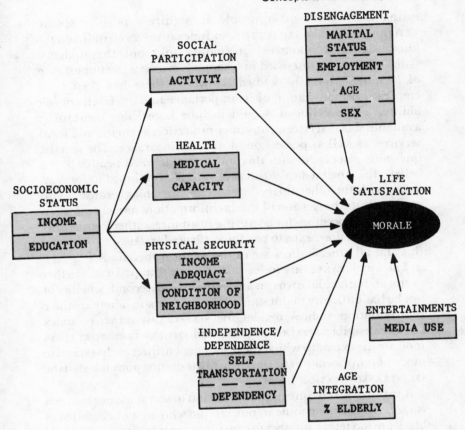

Figure 3.1 Operationalized Model of Life Satisfaction

relationships indirectly affcting life satisfaction. This set of variables certainly does not exhaust the possible influences on life satisfaction. However, together with the variables in the operationalized model, it does include a broad spectrum of those social and economic conditions that constitute the life experiences of older people, as well as some key individual attitudes through which such experiences are filtered.

The first of the additions is SOCIAL ATTITUDE. This index measures the level of a respondent's desire for social contact with other people. A positive interest in a neighborhood center, a desire to see more of friends, relatives, and neighbors, and a preference for eating meals with other people all signify a positive SOCIAL ATTITUDE score. The ABILITY TO COPE index involves an individual's knowledge and resources for finding solutions to problems. Gubrium's work, discussed in Chapter 2, suggests the importance of "coping," broadly defined. However, there has been little empirical demonstration of its importance to date. High coping ability, as we define it, would include knowledge concerning available social services, consumer protection agencies, and legal services, as well as possession of medical insurance. The specific questions associated with this index appear in Appendix B. We believe that the medical insurance variable combined to form an index with the other three "knowledge" variables because it also represents the possession of special information, namely information about procedures for acquiring insurance, rather than simply possession of the means to pay for it. (Procedures used to construct this and all other indices are explained in Appendix A.)

The AUTO OWNERSHIP index includes two things: first, whether or not an individual owns an automobile; and, second, whether or not he has difficulty maintaining it in good repair. There are three transportation indices besides the SELF-TRANSPORTATION index already described. WALK-, PUBLIC-, and OTHERS-TRANSPORTATION indicate the extent to which the respondent utilizes each respective mode of transportation in traveling to the destinations listed in the SELF-TRANSPORTATION index.

A variable given considerable attention in social science research is race. Non-white people in our sample who are not classified as black are too few in number to constitute a valid third category and are omitted from the analysis. Therefore, the variable RACE signifies either black or white. RELIGIOSITY indicates whether or not a person believes in a life after death, and measures the strength of that belief when it is present. As a result, we are in fact measuring the devoutness of a person within the specific context of the traditional Christian belief-system because this context predominates in the society we are studying.

The last three variables to be discussed here involve the residential proximity of relatives and signficiant others. NUMBER IN HOUSEHOLD refers to the number of other people living in the same household as the respondent, and because of this measure, we also are able to distinguish between those respondents who are LIVING WITH SOMEONE and those who are living alone. KC AREA RELATIVES simply records the number of relatives living in the greater Kansas City metropolitan area, while KC AREA CHILDREN indicates whether or not a respondent has children living in that same area.

Having defined the variables, we have yet to describe the manner in which they are treated in the analysis. However, the description of the analysis will be more meaningful if it is preceded by a discussion of the sample of people interviewed and the city in which they live. So, we will return to the variables after considering the people of this study and their general environment.

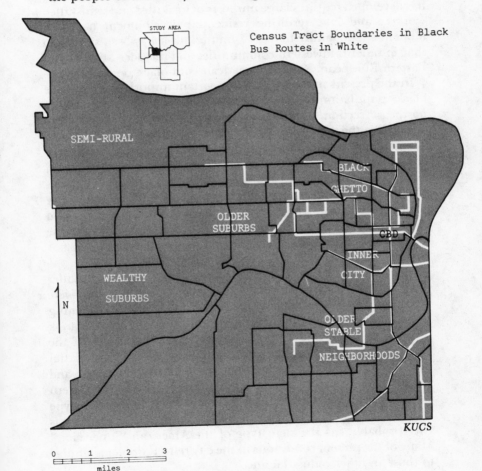

Census Tract Boundaries in Black
Bus Routes in White

STUDY AREA

SEMI-RURAL

BLACK
GHETTO

OLDER
SUBURBS

CBD

INNER
CITY

WEALTHY
SUBURBS

N

OLDER
STABLE
NEIGHBORHOODS

KUCS

0   1   2   3
miles

Figure 3.2 General Map of Kansas City, Kansas

The Environment[2]

Through the years, Kansas City, Kansas, has experienced a fairly steady economic growth. Packing companies and railroads constituted its earliest industries. These industries continued to develop while new ones were added, "until there is at the present time a well-diversified industrial base."[3] The type of industry that has developed requires large numbers of unskilled and semiskilled workers and "the resulting residential development has been modest, single-family homes."[4] Immigration has been similar to that in other midwestern communities and includes Middle- and Eastern-European, Spanish-American, and black populations.

In the present study, the most important minority group is the black population. Traditionally, blacks have settled in the northeast section of the city and while there has been some dispersion, the major portion of blacks still resides in that section. The actual number of blacks has increased substantially over time, but their proportion of the total population has remained relatively constant: in 1890 it was 16.4 percent and in 1970 it was 20.4 percent. In contrast, the next largest non-European minority group are Mexican-Americans who account for between one and two percent of the city's population. The total population of the city in 1970 was 168,213, while population density was 2,961 persons per square mile.

The original town of Kansas City, Kansas, and five smaller communities amalgamated in 1886. Two other communities were incorporated prior to 1930, and further annexation of adjoining areas was gradually undertaken. An important annexation took place in 1966 through which a considerable area west of the existing city was brought within the city limits. Substantial portions of this western area remain sparsely populated and cannot be considered "urban" in the same sense as the eastern sections of the city. In fact, it would more closely fit the stereotype of suburban living. On the other hand, the eastern part of Kansas City probably fits the stereotype of the American "inner city." Many of the present conditions in the city reflect problems similar to those in other industrial areas.

The geographical relationship of Kansas City, Kansas, to the greater metropolitan area has resulted in several special circumstances that should be noted. First, the healthy industrial growth noted earlier is, in part, a product of this city's location within the larger metropolitan area. On the other hand, because of its "proximity to the Kansas City, Missouri, downtown area, the central business district of Kansas City, Kansas, is much less significant and much smaller than would normally be the case for a city of equal population."[5] Further, very high-income residential development has been quite limited in Kansas City, Kansas, primarily because of its proximity to Johnson County, a suburban area on the city's southern border. Johnson County, Kansas, has developed as a high-status residential area which has tended to attract residents seeking prestigious, high-quality homes. The

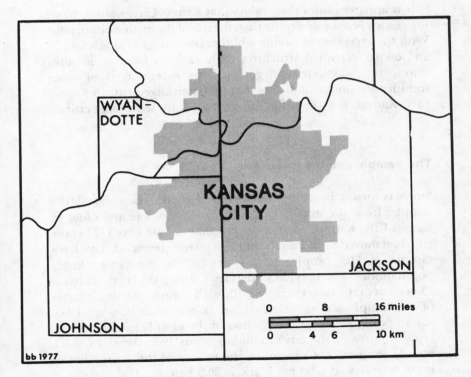

Figure 3.3 Three-County Map

county in 1970 ranked fifth in per capita income among the nation's 3,130 counties and 81st in household income.

The following brief analysis (based on 1970 Census figures) relates Kansas City, Kansas, to its surroundings by comparing three counties in the greater metropolitan area. Wyandotte County includes all of Kansas City, Kansas, plus three small communities on its western border. Johnson County, Kansas, includes a number of suburban communities, the largest of which is Overland Park. Jackson County constitutes the bulk of Kansas City, Missouri, and also contains several smaller communities including Independence, Missouri. It is located immediately to the east of both Wyandotte and Johnson Counties (see area map). Table 3.1 compares selected economic characteristics of these three counties, while Table 3.2 compares selected housing characteristics and Table 3.3, occupational categories.

It is apparent from these tables that Kansas City, Kansas, has a lower socioeconomic profile than the rest of the metropolitan area. With the exception of having a higher percentage of single family and owner occupied structures than Jackson County, it ranks lowest in all selected categories. This exception is of some significance since it indicates that living arrangements in Kansas City, Kansas, are somewhat different from those in large cities.

The Sample and the Interviews

Subjects for the interview survey were selected, via a probability sample, from the total population 60 years of age and older in Kansas City, Kansas. Among the original sample were 177 people who had moved from the city and 36 who were deceased. This left a sample of 705 people, or 2.7 percent of the city's elderly population. Ultimately, 513 interviews were completed, which is 73 percent of the target sample. Although approximately a quarter of the sample was not reached, an examination of several key variables suggests that the portion of the sample interviewed is representative of the city's population. In 1970 the city's black population was 20.4 percent of the total, and the proportion of those interviewed who are black is 20.9 percent. The portion of

Table 3.1   Income

	Wyandotte	Jackson	Johnson
Median Family Income	$9,210	$10,130	$13,384
Percent Families Below Poverty	9.6	7.9	2.9

Table 3.2   Housing

	Wyandotte	Jackson	Johnson
Percent Single Family Structures	75.2	63.9	81.1
Percent Owner Occupied	65.4	58.7	74.8
Median Property Values for Single Family Units	$11,800	$14,900	$22,000
Median Rent	$79	$84	$147

Table 3.3   Occupations*

	Wyandotte	Jackson	Johnson
Percent White Collar	44.2	51.9	70.6
Percent Blue Collar	41.9	34.6	21.1
Percent Service Workers	13.3	13.0	7.5

*The following categories are included in occupational groupings:
  White Collar = Professional/Technical; Manager/Administrator; Sales; Clerical.
  Blue Collar = Craftsmen; Operatives (including transport); Laborers (except farm).
  Service Workers = Service workers and Household workers.

females in the population (60 and over) was 57.8 percent, while females constitute 58.4 percent of those interviewed. Further, the geographical distribution of those interviewed closely approximates that of the city's elderly population. These three variables (race, sex, and age-concentration) enter into the main body of our analysis in rather complex ways. We would like to use them here, however, as a basis for describing our sample in somewhat more detail. For a distribution of the elderly population, see the map on pages 52–53.

Among our sample of respondents, there are few significant differences between blacks and whites in terms of several selected demographic characteristics. Whites, on the average, have slightly more years of formal education than blacks, but the difference is not statistically significant. The mean age of black respondents is 73.1 years, and the mean age of whites in the sample is 72.9 years— also not a significant difference. A few more whites are married, but the difference is not significant. Further, there is not a statistically significant difference in the level of MORALE between black and white respondents. However, there is a significant difference between the races in income size, despite a wide range in the variation of income scores for both groups.

Mean Income	
Blacks	$3,094.
Whites	$4,648.

F = 16.10	p < .01
Standard deviation	= $2,070 for blacks
	= $3,650 for whites

Similarly, there are not many significant differences between males and females in our sample when these same demographic characteristics are considered. Females have slightly higher levels of educational attainment than males, but it is not a significant difference. The difference in average age for males and for females is not significant, although the females in the sample are slightly older. The mean age for females is 73.0 years, while it is 72.8 years for the males. There is a significant difference in MARITAL STATUS, with more males being married than females.

Mean Marital Status*	
Males	1.753
Females	1.410
F = 61.7	p < .01

*1 = not married; 2 = married

A statistically significant difference in income size also occurs between males and females in our sample. Again, the distribution of INCOME is widely dispersed.

Mean Income	
Males	$5,293
Females	$3,560
F = 30.1	p < .01
Standard deviation	= $3,654 for males
	= $3,005 for females

There is no statistically significant difference between males and females in the level of MORALE.

The primary objective of the Kansas City interview survey was to determine the needs of elderly people as they perceive them and as their needs could be inferred from the circumstances in which they live. In developing the interview schedule, we began with the assumption that older people have certain basic needs that pertain to all adults living in this society. Since there are an overwhelming variety of needs, we felt it necessary to develop some reasonable descriptive categories which would help us establish a scheme for selecting questions to be included in the interviews. Therefore, the following categories guided the development of the schedule.

First of all, we posited three main needs that must be fulfilled for the individual's survival, which we termed "maintenance needs." They include: adequate health; sufficient economic resources; and satisfactory interpersonal relations. Sufficient economic resources include the following sub-categories: income; expenses; savings; and insurance. Interpersonal relations include the sub-categories: family; friends; neighbors; and "servicers" (e.g., clerks, waiters, bus drivers, mailmen, etc.). We then posited two categories of what we called "instrumental needs," for they were seen as crucial to the fulfillment of the maintenance needs. The first category includes "capacities" that are more-or-less intrinsic to the individual such as physical mobility, motivation, and realistic goals. The second category includes "opportunities" that are related to the individual's environment and are not strictly controlled by him. Opportunities include such things as the

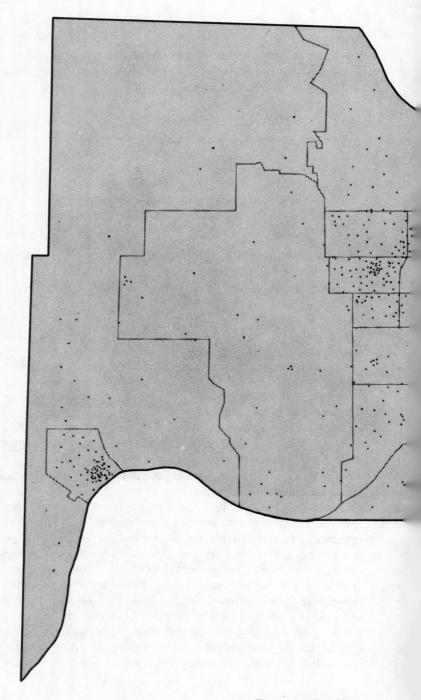

Figure 3.4. Dot Map

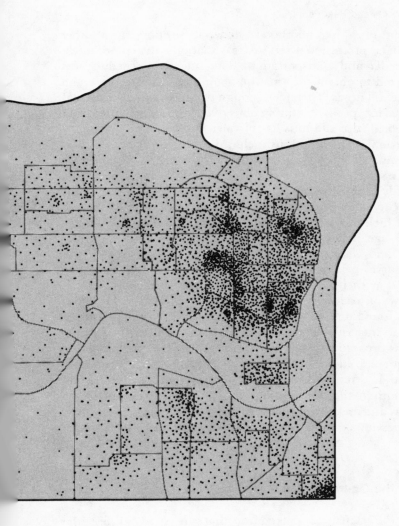

one dot represents five elderly people

100   250   300   500   1000

of Elderly Population

condition of a neighborhood, material support from other individuals, professional services, associations, the communications media and transportation. The interview schedule was constructed to obtain information about these maintenance and instrumental needs. Therefore, though the interview schedule was developed for specific planning objectives, it was constructed from a theoretical base and thus has broader implications.

A portion of the questions included in the interview focus on conditions specific to the Kansas City area, but most are of a more general nature. Some of these latter questions were adapted from previously published studies having objectives similar to the Kansas City survey.[6]

All of the interviewers were mature adults, most being over 50 years of age. They were required to attend periodic training sessions and were continually supervised throughout the two-month survey period. A considerable amount of information was requested at each interview (139 questions); and, consequently, interviews lasted longer than is generally recommended. However, we soon found that, as we had anticipated, elderly people enjoyed talking to interviewers, and we received no complaints about the interview procedure. In addition, we had instructed interviewers to pay particular attention to the respondent's physical condition; and should the respondent appear tired or appear to have difficulty concentrating, the interviewer was instructed to terminate the interview and make an appointment to complete it at a future date. Most interviews took between 60 and 90 minutes to complete.

Testing the Operationalized Model

All of the statistical procedures that are used to test the operationalized theoretical model (and all subsequent models) are explained in detail in Appendix A. This model is tested through a path analysis that includes not only the variables found in the operationalized model but also the remaining variables in our data set. In essence, path analysis—which is based on stepwise multiple regression—tests the causal ordering of the variables in a theoretically closed system. Within each closed system, the combination of independent variables will explain a certain proportion of the variance found in the dependent variables (the explained variance for all path models can be found in Appendix C). In the graphic models representing the systems in the study, the arrows between each pair of variables indicate the direction of influence. The numbers along the arrows are the betas and, therefore, indicate the strength of association between the two variables, either negative or positive. Ambiguous (that is, reciprocal) relationships are designated by curved lines with arrowheads at both ends. The numbers along such curved lines are Pearson correlation coefficients (r). Since each path model is a closed system, the sizes of the betas are affected by the number of variables significantly related to the dependent variable—the larger the number of significantly related variables, the smaller the betas.

The data set we have constructed in order to test the dynamics of life satisfaction is grounded in the respondents' experiencing of old age. Yet, it is obvious that all aspects of the elderly person's world are not included in the data set. So, we should pause a moment to consider the boundaries of our analysis. The percentage of explained variance associated with each model in our analysis is a numerical indication of the proportion of the "old person's world" included in the model. In the case of the Morale Model, slightly over one quarter of the variance in MORALE is accounted for. What does this mean in terms of representing an older person's experiential world? Our focus in this book is the interaction between the elderly person and his social, economic, and to some extent physical environment. Considering the comprehensiveness of the social and economic indicators incorporated in this study, the variance explained in the Morale Model represents, we believe, the major portion of the potential social and economic influences on morale. In this sense, then, the model is replete.

On the other hand, what of the variance left unexplained by the Morale Model? Our data set does not take into account such factors as the genetic structure or the physiology of individuals, early childhood experiences, or many psychological factors, although we have included a few key attitudinal variables. Each of these factors (and of course there would be others as well) could be expected to account for a proportion of the variance in an ideal morale model. But such factors are outside the purview of this study.

Part of our data set derives from responses to open-ended questions, some of which bear upon the question of whether or not people are relatively happy and satisfied with their lives. As explained on pages 41 and 42, we constructed a measure which we have termed PERSONAL SATISFACTION. The correlation between this measure and MORALE turned out to be .336 which is statistically significant but means that only 11 percent of the variance in the two variables is accounted for by the relationship between them. Apparently, they are similar measures to a limited extent but are by-and-large measures of different dimensions of life satisfaction. To examine the possible dimensions they represent, we compare them using stepwise multiple regression analysis in which all other variables in our data set are treated as independent variables.

As shown in Table 3.4, four of the (statistically significant)

Table 3.4   Comparison: MORALE and PERSONAL SATISFACTION

Results when including all independent variables significant at .05:

Independent Variable	Morale Beta	Personal Satisfaction Beta
Activity	.17	.16
Self Transport.	.17	---
Medical	.17	.32
Cond. of Neigh.	.11	.09
Capacity	.12	---
Ability to Cope	.10	---
Income Adequacy	.12	.12
Percent Elderly	.09	---
Income	.09	---
Dep. on Family	---	.13
Dep. on Fr. & Neigh.	---	.10
Media Use	---	- .09
KC Area Children	---	.09
Social Attitude	---	- .07
Variance Explained	.27	.24
Residual	.85	.87

Table 3.5   Comparison: MORALE and PERSONAL SATISFACTION

Results after deleting common independent variables:

Morale Beta		Personal Satisfaction Beta	
Capacity	.25	KC Area Children	.12
Ability to Cope	.19	Dep. on Fr. & Neigh.	.10
Self Transport.	.18	Dep. on Family	.07
Percent Elderly	.09	Media Use	− .07
Income	− .02	Social Attitude	− .05
Variance Explained	.20		.03
Residual	.89		.98

variables influencing MORALE also influence PERSONAL SATISFAC-
TION. At the same time, each dependent variable has a set of five
independent variables unique to it. The results shown in Table 3.5
constitute a comparison between the two dependent variables after
the independent variables common to both have been deleted. The
variables unique to PERSONAL SATISFACTION constitute a dimension
of life satisfaction which might best be described as the availability
of potentially supportive persons.[7] This availability is related to
life satisfaction in all likelihood because it engenders a sense of
security in the face of possible emergencies. However, the most
important thing to be noted about this dimension is that it
accounts for only 3 percent of the variance in the PERSONAL
SATISFACTION model while the "common" variables account for 21
percent. In the MORALE model, the "common" variables explain 7
percent of the variance while the "unique" variables explain 20
percent. Thus, we see in the "unique" dimension of PERSONAL
SATISFACTION social factors that are not included in the morale
measure; but, their impact is comparatively slight. The MORALE
measure, then, is by far our best indicator of life satisfaction.

Let us turn now to a consideration of the Morale Model
presented in Figure 3.5. How does this model, which reflects the
results of a path analysis, compare with the Operationalized
Theoretical Model appearing on page 43? First of all, one of the
least emphasized variables in the gerontological literature on life

satisfaction enters the Morale Model. The variable is ABILITY TO
COPE, which represents the extent of a person's knowledge for
resolving certain types of problems. It is possible that such
problem-solving ability has been neglected as a source of life
satisfaction because old people generally have been regarded as
essentially passive, simply reacting to circumstances over which
they have little control, rather than as active problem solvers.

While there is only one *new* variable involved in the Morale
Model, four of the variables hypothesized from the literature failed
to appear among these interrelationships; and the ordering of
relationships we see here is quite different from that predicted in
the operationalized model. Of the four variables failing to appear,
EMPLOYMENT and MEDIA USE drop out of the path analyses entirely,
but MARITAL STATUS and DEPENDENCY (more distantly related to
MORALE than those variables in Figure 3.5), reappear later in the
study. EMPLOYMENT and MARITAL STATUS having dropped out of the
Morale Model, the only remaining components of the "disengagement" cluster are AGE and SEX. The only influence of AGE on
MORALE is through CAPACITY, while SEX has a more diffuse impact
on MORALE, but only through other variables.

The indicators of socioeconomic status behave differently from
the behavior predicted for them in the hypothetical model. INCOME
impacts positively on MORALE only through INCOME ADEQUACY. Its
direct influence on MORALE is negative. This is a surprising
finding, and we will discuss it at length in Chapter 5. EDUCATION
does not relate directly to MORALE but only through ACTIVITY and
ABILITY TO COPE. Considering these findings, as well as the fact that
financial condition does not impact directly on the health
variables, it appears that socioeconomic status has a more
restricted, though in some ways a more complex, relation to life
satisfaction than predicted.[8]

It should be noted that there are relatively few links among the
primary variables (those impacting directly on MORALE). ABILITY
TO COPE is linked with ACTIVITY and ambiguously with INCOME
ADEQUACY. The most diffuse effect emanates from CAPACITY which
influences MORALE directly and indirectly through four other
primary variables. CAPACITY and MEDICAL, as well as MEDICAL and
MORALE, are related ambiguously. The role of CAPACITY in life
satisfaction, along with that of ABILITY TO COPE, MEDICAL, and

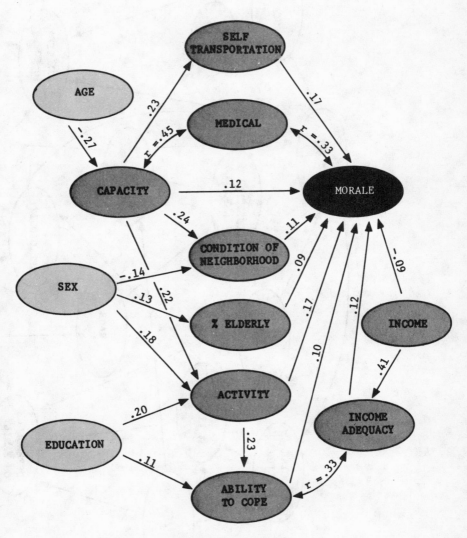

Figure 3.5 Morale Model

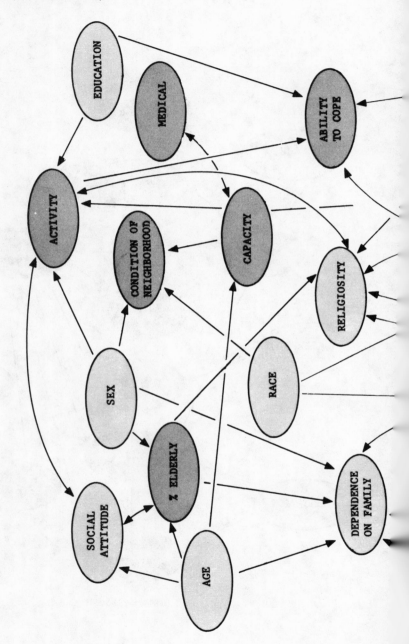

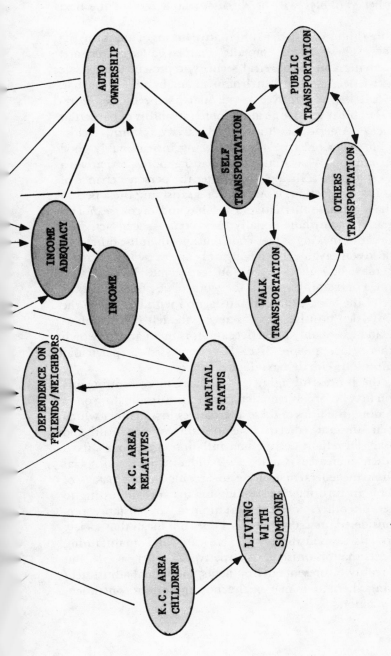

Figure 3.6 Secondary Relationships

several other variables will be discussed at length in the next chapter.

In essence, Figure 3.5 depicts alternative means of attaining life satisfaction. These rather broadly defined alternatives are: problem-solving ability; physical security, represented by a safe and attractive neighborhood environment and by an income that, regardless of size, is perceived as adequate; self-reliance, represented by the ability to drive an automobile, an ability of particular significance in American culture; social activity; residing in close proximity to other older people; and being in reasonably good physical condition. We would expect that the more alternatives a person is capable of realizing, the greater the person's chance of achieving life satisfaction. However, for a satisfying life a person need not have all these alternatives available; and, of course, not all the alternatives contribute equally to MORALE—social activities and self-reliance making larger contributions than the others. In fact, it is also conceivable that having only one or two alternatives available may be sufficient for an acceptable level of life satisfaction. For example, one of the women we portrayed at the beginning of the book expressed satisfaction with her life on the basis of only two positive circumstances: she felt her neighborhood safe and reasonably attractive, and it is in an area in which many other older people live. She expressed a particular attachment to one elderly next-door neighbor.

Indeed, the process of aging as it relates to continuing life satisfaction may be largely a matter of flexibility in adjusting one's emphasis along the lines of these alternatives in a manner which changing circumstances dictate. If, as an example, one's health and ability to be self-reliant decline and inflation erodes one's fixed income, then increased contact with older people and social participation in general may have to become the mainstays of morale. This in turn may necessitate, for instance, adjusting to dependence on others for transportation, a circumstance previously considered unacceptable. This does not mean that society may shirk its responsibility for creating and maintaining environments that optimize the alternatives of older people. But given the reality of present environments, individual adjustment to decreasing alternatives may be the most important constituent of life satisfaction.

It is not possible to sufficiently understand these alternative paths to life satisfaction without considering the secondary relationships that impinge upon the factors relating directly to MORALE. However, a model displaying the network of secondary relationships would appear as it does it in Figure 3.6. Since this figure is obviously too complicated to discuss intelligibly or even to assimilate successfully, our analysis will proceed by discussing the relationships among conceptually coherent subsets of the variables pictured in it. In all but one case these subsets are derived from variables relating directly to MORALE. The exception centers on two variables indirectly related to MORALE that are constituents of dependency, which is, of course, the obverse of self-reliance which relates directly to MORALE.[9] We should keep in mind throughout the analysis that the subsets of variables are themselves interrelated.

In the next chapter we examine three subsets that more closely relate to the personal dimension of life satisfaction: physical condition, problem solving, and dependency. The subsets that are considered in Chapter 5 reflect, relatively speaking, an environmental dimension of life satisfaction—physical security, age concentration (geographically defined), and transportation.

Notes

1. Robert Dubin, *Theory Building* (New York: Free Press), pp. 234–35.

2. The section on the environment appears in slightly altered form in Forrest J. Berghorn and Ronald C. Naugle, *Changing Residence in Kansas City, Kansas: The Geographic and Socioeconomic Bases of Urban Mobility* (Kansas City, Mo.: Mid-American Urban Observatory, 1973), pp. 8–12.

3. Planning Department, "Historical Profile," Community Renewal Program, Kansas City, Kan., 1969, p. 1.

4. *Ibid.*

5. *Ibid.*

6. Some of the health questions were adapted from Ethel Shanas, "Family Responsibility and the Health of Older People," *Journal of Gerontology*, vol. 15, (October 1960) pp. 408–11; a number of the questions pertaining to interpersonal relations were adapted from Irving Rosow, *Social Integration of the Aged* (New York: Free Press, 1967); and as we have already indicated, the morale scale was

adapted from Margaret Clark and Barbara G. Anderson, *Culture and Aging* (Springfield, Ill.: Charles C. Thomas, 1967).

7. MEDIA USE, of course, does not indicate the existence of supportive persons. However, as MEDIA USE declines, PERSONAL SATISFACTION tends to increase, and it is understandable that this negative association could be part of a cluster of relationships emphasizing the potential for face-to-face personal contact. The negative beta for SOCIAL ATTITUDE is somewhat surprising. However, its Standard Error is almost as large as its Regression Coefficient (in this regression equation), so we do not have sufficient confidence in the sign to offer a further explanation based on this result.

8. If EDUCATION and INCOME had been combined into a single measure, "socioeconomic status," presumably that measure would have shown a significant influence on both ACTIVITY and INCOME ADEQUACY. As it is, however, each indicator of socioeconomic status relates to a different dimension of life satisfaction, and this distinction could only have been made by keeping the indicators discrete.

9. They are DEPENDENCE ON FRIENDS AND NEIGHBORS and DEPENDENCE ON FAMILY.

FOUR

The Personal Dimension of Life Satisfaction

Introduction

Morale is not just an important consideration for elderly people. It is not easy at any age to maintain a happy countenance and an optimistic outlook on life or to sustain a feeling of confidence about one's ability to deal effectively with the demands and vagaries of life. Yet for those of advanced age, maintenance of high morale depends more on different personal capabilities and behavioral responses to changing circumstances than is the case for younger people. Though most of the problems that confront older people are virtually the same as those faced by adults of other ages, older people must find solutions to problems within a social context different from that in which younger people operate.

For example, the death of a spouse can happen to someone at age 25 or at age 75. But the way the event is perceived and the set of responses available to the survivor will be considerably different at the two age levels. A widow of 25, for instance, may discover after a period of bereavement and disruption that there are a variety of alternatives available to her. She may choose to remarry, she may resume a career, or she may go to school and train herself for a new profession. Because her physical mobility is likely to be comparatively high, her choices are not restricted by what is available to her in a limited locale. On the other hand, a 75-year-old widow is not as likely to remarry, has little chance of resuming an old career or starting a new one, and is less mobile. Lopata suggests that an older widow is less likely to have the independence of thought and action necessary for reentering the social milieu as a single person.

> Role shifts assuming ease of entrance through traditional or new occupations are often not possible due to the withering of skills in marital years and to an absence of retraining programs. The proportion of widows to men available for marriage expands dramatically with increased age, although the ideal and expected solution to the non-married state is still remarriage . . . most Chicago interviewees [older women] find the condition of being minus a husband one of loneliness and of definite status loss. Few are able to use their own social roles to build a status equivalent to the one they carried by being married, by being married to that specific husband, and by belonging to various status groups through his social roles.[1]

Similarly, being laid off and being retired both represent the same thing—unemployment. However, the former is generally perceived as a temporary condition to be surmounted even though the person may eventually have to find a new line of work. For the retiree, the unemployed condition is in almost all cases permanent. As the distinguished magazine editor, Paul Woodring, has noted,

> The man or woman who reaches the age of sixty-five in good health suddenly realizes that he faces perhaps twenty years of unemployment—a period as long as infancy, childhood, and adolescence combined. And however much he may enjoy leisure and may have looked forward to vacations during his working years, he knows that this vacation is going to be much too long.[2]

The impact of retirement upon an individual is by no means necessarily one of physical and emotional disintegration. Indeed, the available studies on the subject contradict such expectations. Nevertheless, some individuals do suffer physiologically and psychologically from forced retirement:

> Men and women who are otherwise perfectly healthy sometimes develop headaches, gastro-intestinal symptoms, oversleeping, irritability, nervousness and lethargy in connection with retirement. These

conditions may even manifest themselves before retirement takes place; they can heighten with the confusion of roles, activities and changes in the structure of one's life that develops at the time of retirement; they worsen if one does not find a satisfactory life style and work supplements after retirement. Without the customary defensive value of work, old emotional conflicts may re-emerge, especially if one has been a "workaholic"—addicted to work. Without purpose, a sense of inadequacy can evolve; and apathy and inertia—and what some have called "senile" behavior—may follow unless the condition is prevented or reversed.[3]

The impact of retirement on a person is the result of the interplay of a number of factors—health, economics, breadth of interests, satisfying human relations, among others—and people respond differently to them. In all cases, however, retirement is hardly likely to be an insignificant point of transition in one's life experience.

It is not unreasonable for the 30-year-old person making $15,000 per year to hope that in 10 years he might double or even triple his income. For the elderly person on a "fixed" income, the best that reasonably can be expected is simply to be able to hold his own. Both old and young may suffer serious illness, but there is a much greater likelihood that the younger person will recover completely and resume his life in the same manner as before his illness. The older person is more likely to experience long-term consequences of such an illness. As Mrs. Weiss reported (p. 3), ". . . and I have developed several ailments that I will have the rest of my life."

In regard to morale maintenance, then, the essential difference between the elderly and those of other ages is the necessity of adjusting their expectations and priorities in the context of a narrowing range of alternatives available to them. Unlike the young, a major change in the circumstances of an older person's life generally, although not always, results in the permanent loss of a social role. As we have suggested, the loss of a spouse usually results in the permanent loss of the husband or wife role, and so on. Furthermore, the acquisition of entirely new roles is a much more difficult process for the older person. At the same time, the elderly are not without personal resources. By definition, they have more years of experience than anyone else which provides them with a broader perspective than they ever had. As Mrs. Fremont said (p.

2), ". . . As the years go by you have more experience so you live more fully each day." There are also more practical advantages to having lived a long time. For instance, the elderly are more apt to have completed mortgage payments on their homes which is an important contribution to one's economic and emotional security.

The loss of roles need not adversely affect the level of morale. In the struggle to continue one's preferred and familiar lifestyle, one may compensate for the disappearance of certain roles and the constriction of alternative behavior patterns by shifting priorities to those (fewer) roles and alternatives which one is still capable of performing successfully, whether or not they previously had high priority.

The Capacity and Activity Networks

In the stepwise multiple regression analysis with MORALE the dependent variable, CAPACITY is the first independent variable to enter the regression equation (beta = .34). As the four intervening variables shown in Figure 4.1 enter the equation, however, the size of CAPACITY's impact on MORALE declines with each step (relative to other independent variables) until reaching its low of beta = .11. The greatest portion of CAPACITY's influence on MORALE, then, is through the other variables. We should look, therefore, at the relationship between CAPACITY and these four variables and, in turn, at their relation to MORALE.

It may be recalled that CAPACITY measures a person's ability to perform a graded series of common household tasks and, therefore, in a more general sense it measures a person's physical condition. If we consider the four intervening variables as being relatively broad personal objectives (remaining active and in reasonably good health, the ability to drive an automobile, and living in pleasant surroundings), then one's physical condition takes on instrumental value. In these terms, CAPACITY exerts a much greater influence on MORALE because of its instrumental quality than it does because of any intrinsic quality. To understand adequately ACTIVITY, SELF-TRANSPORTATION, and CONDITION OF NEIGHBOR-HOOD, each must be approached with equal emphasis on an individual and an environmental perspective. One might say that

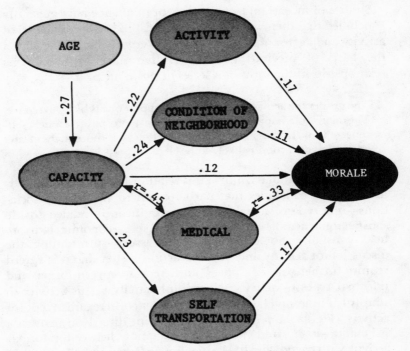

Figure 4.1 Capacity Network

these variables represent an interface between the person and his environment. Such is not the case with the variable MEDICAL health, at least in equal measure. As Figure 4.1 indicates, MEDICAL health has a special, and ambiguous, relationship to both CAPACITY and MORALE; and we will consider it last among the intervening variables.

Possible scores for the ACTIVITY measure range from zero to 12, which means that the mid-point score would be six. The mean of our sample's ACTIVITY scores is 5.4 with a standard deviation of 2.99. This indicates that there is a good deal of variation in the amount of activity engaged in by our sample, and that the average person in our sample is only moderately active. Because of the particular scale that emerged from our Guttman analysis, this measure reflects a special combination of activities (see p. 40) which includes both formal and informal social participation.

Studies of morale and/or adjustment in old age have generally concluded that there is a positive relationship between the level of activity and degree of life satisfaction.[4] Recently Lemon, *et al.*, on the basis of previous activity research have expressed this relationship in the form of a series of postulates:

> The greater the activity, the more role support one is likely to receive. The more role support one receives, the more positive one's self-concept is likely to be. The more positive one's self-concept, the greater one's life satisfaction is likely to be.[5]

Not all activity studies confirm this relationship, however. Cutler, for instance, concludes that participation in voluntary associations—one type of activity—is not significantly related to life satisfaction when the effects of health and socioeconomic status are held constant.[6] Some of the major issues surrounding the discussion of activity and life satisfaction, issues that it is agreed require further research, are: (1) differences between formal and informal types of activity; (2) gainful activity versus activity to simply fill time; and (3) sex and age differences in regard to types of activity. (Figure 4.2 depicts variables relating directly to ACTIVITY.)

Lemon, *et al.* find a modest association between informal activity with friends and life satisfaction (a Gamma of .21), but they find no statistically significant associations between life satisfaction and other kinds of informal activity or any type of formal activity. As we indicate in Chapter 2, Kutner, *et al.* find an association between activity and morale, as do others, but they add the qualification that gainful activity probably promotes higher morale than does activity to fill free time. Maddox finds that "work role maintenance" is related significantly to both activity and morale.[7]

In discussing sex differences in activity as they relate to morale, scholars generally have focused on the retirement experience faced by men and on the impact of widowhood for women. However, Lemon, *et al.* conclude that the loss of these two roles has no significant effect on the relationship between morale and activity, with the exception that a slightly stronger relationship exists between informal activity with friends and the level of life satisfaction among married subjects.[8] Although his study includes both young and old, Booth's conclusions are relevant for us in that

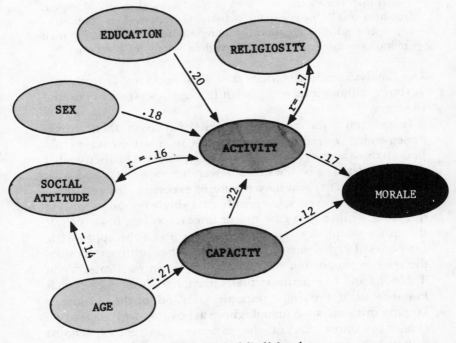

Figure 4.2 Activity Network

they suggest certain expectations about male and female social participation in later years. That is, we would expect from his findings that women would form more nurturant friendships and would be more inclined to participate in expressive voluntary associations.[9] For today's reader, the specific roles and expectations of women discussed in this and other networks may appear somewhat simplistic given the changing status of women. However, it is important to keep in mind the particular status and relatively limited range of experience shared by the cohort of elderly women constituting our sample.

The effect of advancing age on types and levels of activity remains even more uncertain than the other issues. Maddox's analysis,

. . . suggested that low activity may be slightly more predictive of low morale among the younger subjects (below median age [70]) in the panel than among the older ones (median age and above). Moreover, reported *high* interpersonal activity (as opposed to high-*non*-interpersonal activity) appeared more important in predicting high morale among the younger subjects than among the older ones.[10]

Our analysis indicates that AGE does not directly influence ACTIVITY, although its effect is felt through SOCIAL ATTITUDE and CAPACITY.

In addition to the regression analysis of ACTIVITY, there are two "open-ended" questions in the Kansas City interview survey that bear on these activity issues. We asked respondents to discuss what they considered to be life's most rewarding experience and what they considered to be the most rewarding experience for a person in his or her later years. Some people gave single responses to these questions while others gave two or three responses. If we include the entire sample by making judgments about the appropriate categories of experience in which to place the multiple responses, the relative proportion of responses falling in each category in Tables 4.1 and 4.2 remains virtually unchanged from that which is found by using the single responses only. So for the purpose of keeping this analysis as unambiguous as possible, we limit it to the single responses. Six of the experience categories denoted activities, and we related these six activities to the level of the respondent's MORALE. We found no significant difference among the types of activity (formal or informal) in relation to MORALE, either in general or in the later years. However, the distribution of this sample with regard to the types of activity is revealing. Table 4.1 presents the proportion of responses falling in each activity category.

It is apparent from these figures that as a rewarding activity family interaction declines considerably. This suggests that the major source of satisfaction in family interaction during the earlier years was rearing children and otherwise maintaining the family unit. After children have grown and moved from the home, interaction with them is perceived as less rewarding.

While our data do not allow us to test the notion directly, we can speculate upon why the parent-child relationship is less rewarding once the children have grown. Perhaps the main cause is that aging parents at this stage cannot (or fear they soon cannot)

Table 4.1 Sample Distribution by Types of Activity (N=221)

Most Rewarding Activity	General (percent)	Later Years (percent)	Percent Change
Family Interaction	72	12	-60
Hobbies	0.4	29	+29
Church Work	15	40	+25
Neighboring	4	13	+ 9
Employment	8	0	- 8
Association Participation	0	5	+ 5

maintain previous degrees of autonomy and thus prevent at least some role reversal with their children. Clark and Anderson point to this when they say:

> A good relationship with children in old age depends, to a large extent, on the graces and autonomy of the aged parent—in short on his ability to manage gracefully by himself. It would appear that, in our culture, there simply cannot be any happy role reversals between the generations, neither an increasing dependency of parent upon child nor a continuing reliance of child upon parent. The mores do not sanction it and children and parents resent it. The parents must remain strong and independent. If his personal resources fail, then conflicts arise . . . .The ideal situation is when both parent and child are functioning well . . . .Such an ideal situation, of course, is more likely to occur when the parent is still provided with a spouse and where a high socioeconomic status buttresses the parent and child.[11]

These ideal conditions, of course, by no means always prevail, which is why Kutner et al. (1956), could comment some years ago that "As the aging process continues, changes occur in the parent-child relationship, resulting sometimes in complete reversal of the dependency relation."[12] That such change toward greater dependency is a dreaded role alteration is, as Atchley points out, easy to understand:

> We are taught from birth that man's goal in life is to become independent and self-sufficient. This is a deeply ingrained value for

most people, and it is not surprising that [the elderly] are hostile to the idea of giving up their autonomy and become dependent on others.[13]

The successfully adapting parent, say Clark and Anderson, is the one who can accept compensation for lost powers of influence and discipline formerly exerted on children, preferably the compensation of loving respect from children. One can imagine, however, that sweet as such compensation may be, it is often still inadequate to eliminate the pain of having to step aside or stay out of the way of the younger generation.[14]

The potential diminution of pleasure in parent-child relationships may start for parents in middle age. The middle-age parents may see the maturing of their children, as they go off to college or jobs away from home, as signalling the closing of their only avenue to ego-satisfaction and status, or as a threat to their own youthfulness. At this time, too, parents may sense the beginning of the process leading to the "ever widening gulf [which] separates elderly parents from their own mature children."[15]

Streib points to other factors contributing to generational "distance" and consequent decreased satisfaction in parent-child relations. He finds that adult children feel greater positive emotional ties to their families of procreation than to their family of orientation:

> The children . . . having broken some of their emotional ties with their parents and having established new ones with their own conjugal families, do not value so highly their affectional relationships with their parents. . . .There is clearly a difference in the ways the two generations perceive the family situation of parent and child.[16]

Underlying the disparate valuing of affectional relations are generally differences in values and standards about such issues as drinking, housekeeping, child-rearing, manners and etiquette,, and religious beliefs.[17] It is not difficult to imagine that all these differences can be painful to elderly parents at a time in their lives when the maintenance of close affectional ties with children may become increasingly necessary due to a dependency relationship.

When family interaction declines as a rewarding activity, church work and hobbies gain in proportion. The increase in these two activities can be better understood if we compare the responses of men and women in our sample.

Table 4.2   Rewarding Activities by Sex*

Activity	Earlier Years Male (N=88) (percent)	Female (N=125)	Later Years Male (N=97) (percent)	Female (N=110)	Percent Difference Male	Female
Family Interaction	66	74	9	15	-57	-59
Hobbies	1	0	44	16	+43	+16
Church Work	17	15	32	48	+15	+33
Neighboring	6	2	10	16	+ 4	+14
Employment	10	8	0	0	-10	- 8
Association Participation	0	0	4	4	+ 4	+ 4

*Due to independent rounding, totals in Table 4.2 will be slightly different from those in Table 4.1.

A comparison of the changes that took place between the earlier and later years may be more clearly visualized through the graphic presentation of Figure 4.3.

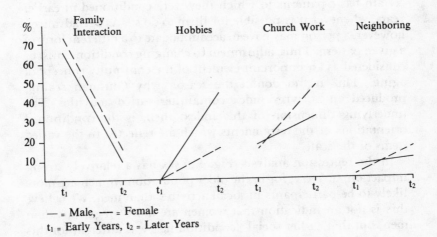

— = Male, ---- = Female
t_1 = Early Years, t_2 = Later Years

**Figure 4.3 Comparison of Selected Rewarding Activities
in the Early and Later Years**

These figures indicate that for both men and women family interaction was the most rewarding experience earlier in their lives, and for both its decline in later years is dramatic. But the activities which replace family interaction in importance are different for men than for women. About three times the proportion of men indicate that hobbies are most important in later years. More than twice the proportion of women, however, find church work most rewarding, and a much greater proportion of women also find neighboring to be most important. One possible explanation for these results is that, after retirement, men withdraw into more solitary pursuits represented by hobbies; while women, after their children have left home, seek greater sociability as represented by church work and neighboring. However, we would like to reiterate our argument that virtually all hobbies have strong social implications. Hobbyists learn about their hobbies from, and often with, other people. Lines of communication with fellow hobbyists are clearly drawn through newsletters, magazines, exhibits, contests, meetings, classes, and so forth.

Because hobbies are not necessarily solitary pursuits, we find the following alternative explanation more compelling. We believe there will be a tendency for people, as they grow old, to continue certain basic patterns to which they were conditioned in earlier years, whenever it is possible for them to do so. As age advances, however, a person may have to accommodate to a different form of a given pattern. Thus, adjustment to changing conditions must be considered as an important element of the continuity concept of aging. This is, no doubt, the reason why Guttman scaling produced an ACTIVITY index containing varied activities. The underlying dimension of this index, then, is the conditioned orientations of the respondents which are reflected in the varied items of the scale.

In the regression analysis (Fig. 4.2) SEX has a relatively strong impact on ACTIVITY, for in the older population women are more likely to be participants in social activities than men. We believe this is not an indication that women are more gregarious than men, but that earlier social "conditioning" was different for this cohort of women. "Men tend to belong to different types of groups than women. Females are more likely to join church and recreation groups, while men join governing boards, job-related and fraternal-service groups."[18] It is comparatively easy for older women to continue participating in activities with which they are familiar, while male participation in job-oriented associations is far more likely to be interrupted by retirement. In Table 4.2 we see that both sexes consider family life to be the most rewarding activity throughout the earlier adult years. For this cohort there is of course a distinction between male and female family roles;[19] the focus for men in earlier years being the "breadwinner" role and for women, the nurturant socialization role.

For many men, whose central concern in earlier life was providing for a family through successful operation in the labor force, life's rewards in later years are conditioned by the value they have learned to place on material manipulation and productivity. Therefore, when the roles they have played in the labor force are no longer open to them, they may either become less active or they may develop new forms of activity. Those men in our sample who presumably have made such adjustments have tended to select activities embodying values similar to those found in occupational roles; that is, they choose hobbies which exemplify instrumental values more than other activities.

Although it may be easier for women than men to continue many of the activities begun earlier in life, adjustments may also be necessary for them primarily because of their often large investment in the child-rearing role. Table 4.2 shows a marked decline in the rewards of family interaction for women, as well as for men, and a corresponding increase in women's involvement in church work and neighboring. This indicates that many women, whose major focus in earlier years was on nurturance and expressive family roles, continue similar orientations in later years but now through participation in these two activities. Women were actually lower than men in the "neighboring" category at the time family roles were dominant. In old age, however, neighboring increases in importance more for women than for men, indicating a continuation of women's expressive orientation when family roles are no longer so rewarding. Most importantly, the value underlying both earlier family interaction and later church participation is that of institution maintenance which, in American society, has traditionally been the responsibility of women. In sum, it is quite likely that activity enhances one's morale to the extent that it allows a continuation of fundamental behavior patterns and value orientations. Such continuation is dependent in large measure on the individual's ability to adjust to new circumstances brought about by the change in role structure associated with advanced age.

In the literature on the social aspects of aging, a great deal is made of retirement and the consequences of being unemployed. If we compare the morale of people in our sample who are working with those who are not, as has generally been done, we find a significant difference in the morale of the two groups.

Table 4.3   EMPLOYMENT and MORALE

Morale	Low	Med. Low	Med. High	High	Total
Working	10	24	22	27	83
Not Working	110	135	90	95	430

X^2 = 9.76 (3 df.) p = .02
Gamma = .274

Those who are working have a higher level of morale than those who are unemployed. At the same time, we found other indications in our data that the relationship between employment and life satisfaction is not so simple. We asked those in our sample who are no longer working (89 percent of the total sample) whether or not they would still like to be working. Sixteen percent said they would prefer being employed, and 84 percent said they would not like to be working anymore. The reason there is a significant difference in the morale of working and non-working people in Table 4.3 is that in this comparison intervening factors are not held constant. People who are working are also relatively healthy, active, and able to cope. They are also younger and virtually all of them drive their own automobiles. For this reason, EMPLOYMENT does not impact on MORALE in our regression analysis where all such factors are held constant. We must conclude, then, that life satisfaction is not a matter of gainful activity versus activities to fill free time. It is, rather, a consequence of continuity and adjustment, as we have suggested above.

Finally, in Figure 4.2 there are two reciprocal relationships with ACTIVITY. The relationship between RELIGIOSITY and ACTIVITY is positive, though weak, because one of the components of the ACTIVITY measure is church attendance. It is difficult to assign a direction to this relationship for the simple reason that having comparatively strong religious beliefs may be a spur to attending church; while on the other hand, attending church, for whatever reason, may tend to strengthen religious beliefs. The same reasoning may be applied to the positive, though weak, relation between SOCIAL ATTITUDE and ACTIVITY. Having a desire for more contact with other people probably motivates a person to be more active; but at the same time, activities, at least of a gratifying nature, might enhance a person's desire for social contact. One might also note that in Figure 4.2 AGE negatively impacts on SOCIAL ATTITUDE. This finding that the desire to be with other people socially tends to decline with advancing age is the only empirical support in our data for disengagement theory.

The second "interface" variable in the Capacity Network is SELF-TRANSPORTATION. Forty-eight percent of the people in our sample have the ability to drive themselves to necessary destinations (and usually do), while 52 percent of the sample is unable to drive. Logically, and in light of some research (e.g., Cutler, 1974), one would expect that having personal automobile transportation would create high morale because it facilitates participation in the activities represented by the ACTIVITY index which themselves impact on MORALE. However, one of the most noteworthy aspects of the Capacity Network (Fig. 4.1) is the absence of a linkage between SELF-TRANSPORTATION and ACTIVITY (at least, our conceptualization but not necessarily others' conceptualizations of activity measures). Thus, it appears that SELF-TRANSPORTATION has an intrinsic capacity to affect life satisfaction independent of social participation. It is our contention that this "intrinsic quality" is self-reliance. Carp reinforces our interpretation when reporting the reaction of retirees to *not* owning and maintaining a car; that is, loss of independence, a loss of autonomy and self-sufficiency, and "indebtedness [to others for rides] which becomes burdensome and demeaning when reciprocation is impossible."[20] Reactions such as these are inimical to high morale. Conversely, then, SELF-TRANSPORTATION can be associated with such high morale-building factors as maintenance of independence, freedom, autonomy, and the ability to reciprocate favors.

Hsu describes self-reliance in the United States as being a "militant ideal which parents inculcate in their children and by which they judge the worth of any and all mankind." But this ideal often conflicts with the reality of the human condition. "In fact, the very foundation of the human way of life is man's dependence upon his fellow men without which we shall have no law, no custom, no art, no science, and not even language."[21] The continued successful maintenance of behavior patterns consistent with cultural values as firmly rooted as self-reliance undoubtedly contributes to a sense of life satisfaction. Continued maintenance of self-reliant behavior, however, must always be a struggle—and perhaps ultimately a losing battle—since it runs counter to the physiological and social contingencies of the human life-cycle. Clark describes the consequences of this struggle in regard to American intergenerational relations.

> The parent must remain—or, at least, appear to remain—strong and independent. This independence is sustained at the price of ever-increasing social distance, and in many American families social relationships between generations are formal and dispassionate. Those who can sustain the semblance of complete self-reliance in this way have higher morale and self-esteem than those who cannot. They may be lonely and in need, but they are at least remaining true to their most cherished ideals.[22]

A number of respondents in the Kansas City survey indicated that personal independence was either still a goal in life for them or one of the most rewarding things about life in their later years. For instance, Mr. Yarbrough, one of our respondents, laments, "I wish I could be working so I wouldn't have to depend on anybody for anything." He also illustrates the independence-dependence paradox when he says, "I just wish I had enough help to get along in life independently." Several other respondents indicate that an important objective for older people is, "to take care of themselves *the best they can*,"[23] which suggests that, for them, it is better to be poor and in need than to be dependent.

In the United States, nothing embodies the cultural value of personal independence any more than the automobile. Above all machines, at least, the automobile symbolizes a modern American's ability to "do for himself," to achieve, and to consume. Thus, we believe that SELF-TRANSPORTATION accurately reflects a major dynamic of morale maintenance for old people living in a society where a premium is placed on personal autonomy and on consumer achievement. The adjustments necessary for those who no longer can transport themselves by driving an automobile are discussed at length in Chapter 5.

The neighborhood environment as it relates to life satisfaction is also emphasized in the next chapter; but we will deal here with a few aspects of neighborhood condition that are pertinent to the personal dimension. Since the neighborhood in which one lives is closely connected to one's self-image, it is evident that a perception of safety and a feeling that the neighborhood presents a good appearance should contribute to high morale. The relationship between CAPACITY and CONDITION OF NEIGHBORHOOD is not as evident, however. To examine this relationship, we selected the 20 percent of our sample with the lowest CAPACITY scores and recorded their perceptions of the safety and appearance of their neighborhoods. We also accounted for male and female differences regarding these perceptions.

Table 4.4   CAPACITY and CONDITION OF NEIGHBORHOOD

	Day		Night		Appearance	
	Safe	Unsafe	Safe	Unsafe	Good	Poor
Male	33	11	11	32	34	6
Female	29	16	9	35	37	7
Total	62	27	20	67	71	13

Men and women with low CAPACITY perceive their neighborhoods in virtually the same way. Both find their neighborhoods particularly unsafe at night and both are generally pleased with the appearance of their neighborhoods. The foremost personal incapacities cited as the reasons for feeling unsafe are poor eyesight and relative immobility. The most frequent environmental factor mentioned is a rather diffuse anxiety about crime in the streets. "I'm afraid of being beat up and robbed." "It isn't safe at night— too much slugging." "The streets are not light enough and are not patrolled enough." "There are too many young punks out at night." These are just a few of the comments about unsafe neighborhood environments. In a number of cases, taverns were associated with unsafe conditions.

At the same time, Figure 5.3, p. 117, shows us that SEX is related to CONDITION OF NEIGHBORHOOD in that women tend to rate their neighborhoods lower than men. The apparent inconsistency in terms of sex differences in these two sets of findings is resolved by considering the influence of CAPACITY. Given adequate levels of capacity and the same neighborhood environment, women can be expected to be more apprehensive about their potential to protect themselves at night than men. As the capacity of both men and women declines (in the case of the present sample because of advancing age), men's perceptions of their ability to protect themselves declines more markedly than is true for women. Thus, for a sample of low CAPACITY people, we find practically no difference between the sexes. In other words, as a man's capacity diminishes, his perceptions about his safety become more like those of women. We would conclude that aging, since it entails declining capacity, tends to override some sex differences that existed earlier in life. This is a conclusion not entirely consistent with continuity theory, especially for men, for it suggests that age itself creates distinct conditions which modify individual perceptions and behavior.

Although most of CAPACITY's impact on MORALE is exerted through intervening variables, a minor portion is direct. A close examination of a few appropriate cases suggests that this direct impact is the result of CAPACITY's association with MORALE among those respondents with the lowest CAPACITY scores. CAPACITY, as we have seen, exerts a facilitating influence on the intervening variables, but when it is extremely low, CAPACITY loses its instrumental role while becoming the dominant determinant of MORALE. When performing such tasks as making the bed or preparing a meal becomes so difficult that they consume all of a person's emotional energy, the locus of a person's problems becomes clearly defined as physical disability *per se* rather than the attainment of broader objectives represented by the intervening variables. The importance that CAPACITY assumes in influencing MORALE when a person no longer feels capable of performing routine daily chores is illustrated by the comments of one of our respondents, Sarah Harkness: "The most difficult thing about life is not being able to do for yourself. I'm not able to work. I can't get out anymore. I can't drive my car, and I can't even do my housework or anything else anymore." Mrs. Harkness' score on the CAPACITY index is among the lowest in the sample, and it is not surprising that her MORALE score is also among the lowest. She summarized her feelings about her condition when she replied, "The thing I need now to make my life better is a new body."

The validity of self-ratings of their medical health by elderly people is a prominent issue in social gerontology. As summarized by Tissue, the subject revolves around the relationship between self-rated health and actual physical condition. Some researchers contend that self-ratings are more a measure of morale than of physical condition, although Tissue finds that, "Such ratings are associated most closely with other indicators of health (objectively and subjectively defined) rather than with general considerations of morale or self-image."[24] At the same time, he stresses that self-rated health is not a reliable index of specific physiological conditions. Our findings, we believe, help to clarify the nature of health which is measured by self-ratings.

As we have pointed out in Chapter 3, our measure of medical health consists of a response generally defining the state of the person's health as he perceives it and four responses focusing on indicators of more specific health problems. The correlation between the general response (i.e., self-perceived health) and the set of four specific indicators is .632.[25] This suggests that while there is a strong relationship between the subjective perception of health and the more objective evaluations, the correspondence is far from exact. Any discrepency between a person's perception of his health and his report of specific health problems may be accounted for by his level of morale. That this is so is indicated by the findings that: (1) there is a .344 correlation between the variables MEDICAL and MORALE; and (2) there is no relationship between MEDICAL and AGE (see Fig. 4.1). There is no question that, objectively, health declines with advancing age. However, physical decline is not uniform among all old people nor is it perceived uniformly. And one of the major influences on how health is perceived is the more generalized feeling of life satisfaction. (It should be remembered that this relationship is reciprocal and that the objective level of health will also influence a person's life satisfaction.)

Figure 4.1 also shows that the CAPACITY measure of physical condition is decidedly affected by AGE. As people advance in age their capacity to accomplish everyday tasks declines. The reason that MEDICAL and CAPACITY behave differently with respect to AGE is that MORALE influences MEDICAL but not CAPACITY. Whereas a person may view his health as reasonably good (given his layman's expectation of health in old age and his evaluation of the medical condition of his peers), when he is asked to judge his capacity to perform specific tasks, his layman's understanding of himself is far more authoritative than it is with respect to his medical condition. Therefore, it may be easier to report good health, relative to generalized perceptions of self and others, than it is to report enduring capacities in the face of daily experience. Table 4.5 provides a comparison of the effect of AGE on CAPACITY and on MEDICAL health. It accentuates the difference between the two indices. The "high MEDICAL" group and the "high" and "medium CAPACITY" groups have virtually the same mean age. The mean age for the "medium MEDICAL" group is older than for the "medium CAPACIY" groups while the "low CAPACITY" group is considerably older than the "low MEDICAL" group. This supports the idea that

Table 4.5   The Effect of AGE on MEDICAL and CAPACITY

Low CAPACITY Group	76.1 mean age	
Medium CAPACITY Group	71.6 mean age	
High CAPACITY Group	71.8 mean age	
F ratio = 22.66	p < .01	
Low MEDICAL Group	73.7 mean age	
Medium MEDICAL Group	73.0 mean age	
High MEDICAL Group	71.5 mean age	(BGdf = 2
F ratio = 3.07	p = .05	WGdf = 494)

people evaluate their health relative to their expectations concerning advancing age, since they appear to perceive a slight decline in their health as they get older but then reconcile themselves to the health problems of age. When health problems obstruct CAPACITY, however, there is no denying these consequences.

These various findings indicate that the most reliable index for ascertaining a person's physical condition, *per se*, is CAPACITY.[26] Its decline would not be the result of social or psychological changes, such as role loss (e.g., retirement, widowhood), but would occur for strictly physical reasons. On the other hand, self-evaluation of one's medical health includes not only the perception of physical decline but also what might be called a general sense of well-being which would not affect the CAPACITY index.

In Edwards and Klemmack's hypothetical model of life satisfaction (see p. 29), socioeconomic status is pictured as influencing morale through health (as well as through informal participation).[27] In our model, socioeconomic factors do not impact on MEDICAL health. We suspect that the recent proliferation of social programs aimed at improving health care, particularly Medicare, has reduced the significance of financial circumstances on medical health care for the elderly.

The Ability to Cope with Problems Network

A high coping score indicates that a person has had the experience of obtaining needed social services and/or that he has the knowledge to deal effectively with consumer, legal, and medical problems should they occur. The ABILITY TO COPE scale ranges from zero to six; the mean score of the sample is 2.4 (also its median) with a standard deviation of 1.3. In a general sense, then, the people in the sample are moderately to poorly prepared to deal effectively with these common problems.

There are two major linkages in the network. One we interpret to be social participation in learning situations (EDUCATION, ACTIVITY) and the other, material resources (INCOME ADEQUACY, AUTO OWNERSHIP, INCOME). MARITAL STATUS can be seen as affecting

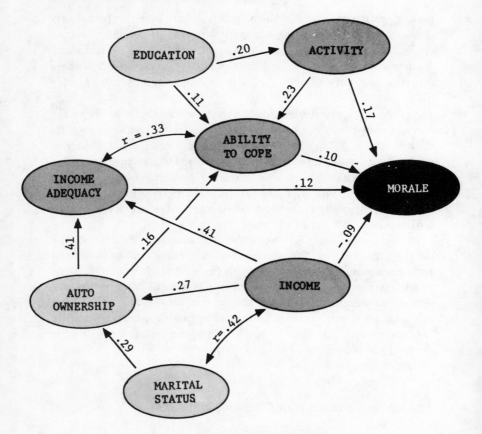

Figure 4.4 Ability to Cope Network

the size of one's income and the likelihood of owning an automobile. In the first linkage, the strongest direct influence on ABILITY TO COPE is ACTIVITY. ACTIVITY, here, is characterized predominantly by social interaction, which provides the context for sharing experiences and information. Thus, a greater degree of activity increases the probability of one's exposure to knowledge useful in problem solving. While we find that it clearly assumes a problem-solving dimension in our data, activity rarely has been associated with problem-solving abilities in the literature on aging. When the relationship between activity and problem solving is mentioned, it is usually indirectly and in passing. For example, Lopata suggests that non-participation of older widows in voluntary associations contributes, among other things, to their very small "life space" and to their "lacking an understanding of the larger world and to their ability to utilize its social resources."[28]

The relationship we find between ACTIVITY and ABILITY TO COPE becomes clearer when we consider that making oneself available for direct communications with others is often essential to learning "what to do." Certainly lack of activity, with its connotation of isolation, would appear to work against sharing of information and insight helpful to problem solving. It is apparent that one of the functions of ACTIVITY in this network is to increase the elderly person's awareness of available social resources for solving problems.

The educational function of social activity is underscored by the fact that EDUCATION, at once, has a substantial influence on ACTIVITY and impacts directly on ABILITY TO COPE. EDUCATION here measures the extent of one's formal schooling where presumably the most basic skills are acquired for dealing with the problems of urban-industrial life. We believe that the relationship between ACTIVITY and EDUCATION indicates more than the apparent conclusion that people who have completed more schooling tend to be more active. It is also quite likely that formal educational attainment, which in itself is training for problem solving, enhances receptivity to and/or use of problem-solving information available in social contact situations.

The linkage involving material resources suggests a second distinct component of coping ability. Gubrium finds that absence among old people of the fear of insolvency (among other fears) correlates with *feeling* competent in coping with life's everyday contingencies.[29] Conversely, then, having adequate material resources would reduce the fear among old people of financial vulnerability, a fear adverse to effective coping. Since our measure of coping entails not perceptions but skills, our findings suggest that the correlation extends beyond feeling to actual outcomes.

We have indicated a reciprocal relationship between INCOME ADEQUACY and ABILITY TO COPE in Figure 4.4. Because the former variable involves, at least in part, management of one's finances, we consider it a subset of the more general phenomenon of coping ability. INCOME, while not impacting directly on COPE, does influence COPE indirectly through INCOME ADEQUACY and AUTO OWNERSHIP. Clearly, owning an automobile enhances a person's ability to deal effectively with a variety of problems because of the increased mobility it allows. It is not unreasonable to assume that the location of assisting agencies and individuals will often be inconvenient to the residences of most elderly citizens. Therefore, the kind of mobility provided by an automobile is a substantial asset in dealing with problems in a modern American city. The relationship among various material resources is considered at greater length in the next chapter.

Finally, we would suggest that the mechanism through which coping ability affects life satisfaction is a person's self-image. While ABILITY TO COPE is defined as a set of skills, possessing such skills is bound to produce a general feeling of efficacy and control over one's life, thus enhancing a person's self-image. The more positive a person's self-image, the higher we would expect his morale to be.[30].

The Dependency Network

Dependency is not only the obverse of self-reliance but is in itself a major issue in social gerontology. Dependency is defined by Clark as, " . . . the extent to which the means necessary for survival are not directly available to the individual through his own efforts, but must, to some extent, be obtained from others."[31] In a modern, urban society, survival depends not on material sustenance alone, but also on socio-emotional support. Thus, while material support can come from a variety of sources—state welfare mechanisms, municipal agencies, and private organizations, as well as family, friends, and neighbors—socio-emotional support comes almost exclusively from significant others with whom one interacts on a personal basis. The two major areas of possible dependency covered in this network (DEPENDENCE ON FAMILY and DEPENDENCE ON FRIENDS AND NEIGHBORS) include both material and socio-emotional support though they do not include basic income maintenance, which in a modern society is covered to one degree or another by other sources.

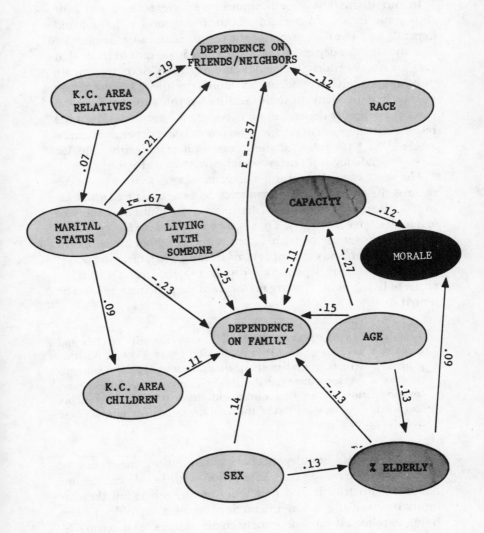

Figure 4.5 Dependency Network

In our discussion of self-reliance, we have pointed out how important it is to Americans, both young and old, to avoid dependency. Twenty percent of the people in our sample indicate that they are not dependent on family and 50 percent indicate that they are not dependent on friends and neighbors. Sixty percent are only moderately dependent on family, while 20 percent are extremely dependent on their families. At the same time, only 5 percent are highly dependent on friends and neighbors. Given the resistance to dependency, those who report being dependent can be assumed to have reported their condition realistically, and for them dependency is a crucial social-psychological issue.

The set of variables leading to DEPENDENCE ON FAMILY is not the same as the set leading to DEPENDENCE ON FRIENDS AND NEIGHBORS. In fact, the two focal points of dependency are mutually exclusive to a high degree (r = -.57). That is, a person tends to be dependent either on his family or on his friends and neighbors, but not on both. Rosow appears to support this finding when he writes about old people who are dependent ("disadvantaged," as he puts it, by virtue of living alone, having no local children, being widowed or retired or sick):

The frequency of contact with children and that with friends and neighbors have no *general* reciprocal effect on each other. But this general pattern is subject to sharp qualifications for disadvantaged persons. . . . Among these specifically disadvantaged aged, there is an inverse relationship between contact with children and with neighbors and friends. As they see less of their children, they see more of their friends and neighbors.[32]

In other words, non-dependent social relations need not be mutually exclusive—that is, interaction with family on the one hand or with friends and neighbors on the other; but they are mutually exclusive when interaction involves an older person living in relatively more dependent circumstances. As noted above, most dependent relationships among our sample involve the family. Quite likely, it is only when the family is inaccessible or non-existent that most elderly people turn to friends or neighbors for assistance of a continuing nature.

It may be noted in Figure 4.5 that the existence of relatives in the Kansas City area is negatively related to DEPENDENCE ON FRIENDS

AND NEIGHBORS, while existence of children in the area is positively related to DEPENDENCE ON FAMILY. Also when there is a high concentration of older people in the neighborhood environment, there is a tendency for these older people to be less dependent on their families (note the negative relationship between % ELDERLY and DEPENDENCE ON FAMILY). At the same time, the high concentration of older peple in a neighborhood does not have the positive effect on DEPENDENCE ON FRIENDS AND NEIGHBORS that would be expected given the above negative relationships.

The absence of dependency on friends and neighbors is most simply explained by the culturally induced aversion to dependence of any form. However, when dependence becomes unavoidable, the least culturally stigmatized type of dependency is between an individual and his family. While the accessibility of relatives lessens dependence on friends and neighbors, and children are the relatives old people turn to most frequently for assistance, the extent of an older person's dependence on his children will be affected by their geographic proximity. The areas of high elderly concentration in the city are in general the older, poorer, and more densely populated areas. There is, no doubt, a tendency for the children of elderly people to live elsewhere in the city along with other younger families. If the children do not live nearby, the parent is less likely to be dependent on them.

A further indication that the family, not friends or neighbors, assumes the principal responsibility for dependent elderly people is the association between DEPENDENCE ON FAMILY and CAPACITY. When CAPACITY declines to a level at which one can no longer maintain everyday living habits, it falls to family members to provide the necessities of life for the older person. The assisting role of family members perhaps is predictable, given the literature on the importance of the extended family in the lives of old people and the strong functioning relations between the aged and their children in the United States and other modernized societies.[33] Furthermore, Shanas reports that (for her sample) the "sicker" the old person, the greater the likelihood of his living close to at least one child.[34] We also believe that assistance from one's family does less violence to the older person's sense of independence than would be the case if it were necessary to impose upon a friend or neighbor. Weiss notes that provision of services or the making available of resources is a primary theme in kin relationships.[35]

An alternative explanation for the absence of a positive relation between age concentration and dependency on friends and neighbors (while age concentration impacts negatively on family dependency) involves a psychological dimension to dependency. Although we are not able to test this explanation directly in our analysis, we would like to suggest the possibility that just as a general sense of well-being may affect a person's perception of his health, so too might a general sense of satisfactory interpersonal relations affect a person's perception of his dependency. If a person receives assistance from someone but is physically and/or otherwise capable of returning favors, such *mutual* dependency may allow the individual to retain a sense of self-reliance. Under a set of special circumstances, such a reciprocal relationship could obtain between an old person and his family, but it is far more likely to occur between age-mates who live in close proximity. In other words, assistance given and received among older neighbors will not manifest itself in a relation between % ELDERLY and DEPENDENCE ON FRIENDS AND NEIGHBORS.

Judging from the relationships depicted in Figure 4.5, the most important bulwark against dependency is marriage.[36] Married status, of course, may be thought of as constituting a continuous dependency relationship. From the beginning of marriage, a traditional division of labor renders one spouse to some degree dependent on the other. This form of dependency, however, is viewed by the couple and by society in general as a "natural" contractual arrangement which stigmatizes neither person. Since being married usually means that a person is living with someone, there is an obvious and strong relationship between these two variables. However, while being married is negatively related to DEPENDENCE ON FAMILY, living with other people is positively related to it. This positive association indicates that for many people who are dependent on their families, dependency takes the form of living with the family member or members.

At the same time, remaining married in old age is relatively difficult since the probability of losing one's spouse increases, especially for women. While women are less likely to remain married in later life than men, they are more likely to be dependent on their families and may be less inclined than men to feel the stigma attached to loss of independence. Given the period in which the women in our sample grew up, virtually all of them would have learned to accept a more dependent role within the family, and therefore would feel less reluctant later in life to call upon family members for assistance.

We have seen thus far that SEX enters into our analysis through several networks of relationships impacting on life satisfaction. Women in our sample are more dependent on their families than men, a condition which likely represents, for this cohort of women, continuity with previous roles and patterns of behavior. We have also seen that women are more likely to be participants in social activities than men. We have suggested that it may be easier for older women to continue their participation in activities with which they are familiar, while male participation in job-oriented associations is more likely to be interrupted by retirement. This would suggest that continuity with previous behavior may be more easily maintained by older women than by older men. However, our analysis of satisfying activities in the earlier and later years reveals that, while the form of the activity may change, both men and women continue in later life the same underlying activity orientations that they had developed in previous years. As we will see in Chapter 5, SEX is related to the age-concentration variable % ELDERLY. That is, women tend to live in areas of the city that are characterized by higher densities of elderly persons. This situation is largely a result of the phenomenon of "aging-in-place." While we will discuss this relationship in greater detail in the next chapter, it may be noted here that "aging-in-place" also represents for older women another type of continuity with previous personal experience. As we have indicated in our discussion of the relationship between SEX and CONDITION OF NEIGHBORHOOD, women tend to rate their neighborhoods lower than men, but men with low CAPACITY perceive their neighborhoods as negatively as women do. While women may always have been more apprehensive than men about their ability to protect themselves, men become more fearful as their capacity to protect themselves declines with advancing age. Thus, we see a measure of continuity in the perceptions of women, but a change in the attitudes of men. This finding suggests that advancing age tends to obscure a sex difference that may have existed for our sample in their earlier years.

Our findings indicate, then, that it may be somewhat easier for older women to maintain a greater degree of continuity with previous personal experience than it is for older men who retire from jobs and cease participation in job-related associations, and who may experience a more precipitous decline in their perceived ability to protect themselves. At the same time, these findings indicate the complex interplay between continuity with past experience and the special demands and contingencies of old age that necessitate individual adjustment. We will consider further the themes of continuity and special status characteristics of old age in Chapter 6.

Unexpectedly, RACE directly impacts on DEPENDENCE ON FRIENDS AND NEIGHBORS, though not on DEPENDENCE ON FAMILY. That is, blacks more than whites tend to be dependent socially and/or psychologically on their friends and neighbors. The simplest explanation for this finding would be that blacks have fewer relatives in the Kansas City metropolitan area to whom they can turn for assistance. A test of this hypothesis is presented in Table 4.6.

Table 4.6   Relatives and Children in the Kansas City Area by Race

	Mean Relatives in KC Area	Mean Children in KC Area
Blacks	1.61	.470
Whites	1.65	.612
F ratio	0.086 (N.S.)	6.633 (P = .01)

There is no significant difference in the number of all types of relatives living in proximity to blacks as compared to whites. However, white respondents have significantly more children living near them. And as we have indicated previously, children are the relatives old people turn to most often for assistance.

Again, there is an alternative explanation that involves the psychological dimension of dependency. Cameron *et al.* suggestively report that blacks claim to feel liked by the "generalized other" more than whites claim to feel liked by the "generalized other."[37] By this he means that blacks (who in a segregated society live and interact predominantly with other blacks) feel more liked by those around them than do whites. Since it is reasonable to assume that people prefer to depend on others by whom they feel liked, blacks for this reason may become more dependent than whites on their friends and neighbors. Also, this difference in dependency may represent part of a strategic buffer network of social and psychological interaction with friends and neighbors developed by blacks in order to cope with the strains of minority status in the United States.[38]

An important adjustment in old age is coming to terms with increasing dependency. As we have noted, dependency does not impact on MORALE directly. And it is not surprising to find that dependency in itself is not inimical to life satisfaction, since it is generally recognized that people are dependent to varying degrees on a variety of people throughout the life cycle. Although dependency does not necessarily inhibit good morale, it is likely to do so if the dependent relationship produces a high level of stress for the aged person. For example, a dependent person may feel or may be made to feel that he is a burden on his friends and relatives.

Making adjustments in old age, whether to dependency or to other contingencies, is no easy matter in the face of changing personal circumstances, ingrained cultural prescriptions, and habits which in the past have been personally fulfilling. Yet, the need for adjusting personal goals can stimulate new meaningful perspectives for one's life; and as some observers have theorized,[39] the search for meaning is the *sine qua non* of life satisfaction at any age.

Notes

1. Helena Z. Lopata, "Role Changes in Widowhood: A World Perspective," in Donald O. Cowgill and Lowell D. Holmes (eds.), *Aging and Modernization* (New York: Appleton-Century-Crofts), p. 285.

2. Paul Woodring, "Why 65? The Case Against Mandatory Retirement," *Saturday Review* (August 7, 1976), p. 18.

3. Robert N. Butler, *Why Survive? Being Old in America* (New York: Harper and Row), 1975, p. 72.

4. See particularly George L. Maddox, "Activity and Morale: A Longitudinal Study of Selected Elderly Subjects," *Social Forces*, vol. 42 (1963), pp. 195–204.

5. Bruce W. Lemon, Vern L. Bengtson, and James Peterson, "An Exploration of the Theory of Aging: Activity Types and Life Satisfaction Among In-Movers to a Retirement Community," *Journal of Gerontology*, vol. 27 (1972), pp. 511–23.

6. Stephen J. Cutler, "Voluntary Association Participation and Life Satisfaction: A Cautionary Research Note," *Journal of Gerontology*, vol. 28, no. 1 (1973), p. 99. A later study, Jackie Aucoin and C. Neil Bull, "Voluntary Association Participation and Life Satisfaction: A Replication Note," *Journal of Gerontology*, vol. 30, no. 1 (1975), pp. 73–76, replicates Cutler's study and finds support for Cutler's conclusions that good health and high socioeconomic status, not voluntary association participation *per se*, promote high morale.

7. Lemon *et al.*, *op. cit.*; Maddox, *op. cit.*, p. 201; Bernard Kutner, David Fanshel, Alice Togo, and Thomas S. Langner, *Five Hundred Over Sixty: A Community Survey on Aging* (New York: Russell Sage Foundation, 1956), p. 21.

8. Lemon, *et. al.*, *op. cit.*, p. 518.

9. Alan Booth, "Sex and Social Participation," *American Sociological Review*, vol. 37 (April 1972), pp. 183–92. Our discussion of expressive associations appears on pages 000–000.

10. Maddox, *op. cit.*, p. 201.

11. Margaret Clark and Barbara G. Anderson, *Culture and Aging* (Springfield, Ill.: Charles C. Thomas, 1967), pp. 275–76. Alan C. Kerckhoff, "Family Patterns and Morale in Retirement," in Ida H. Simpson and John C. McKinney (eds.), *Social Aspects of Aging* (Durham, N.C.: Duke University Press, 1966), pp. 173–94, finds high morale in elderly parents associated with "relative independence on the two generations and with a functional home-based pattern of activities on the part of the older couple" (p. 192), thus supporting Clark and Anderson's view of the "ideal situation."

12. Kutner *et al.*, *op. cit.*, p. 19.

13. Robert C. Atchley, *The Social Forces in Later Life: An Introduction to Social Gerontology* (Belmont, Cal.: Wadsworth, 1972), p. 107.

14. Clark and Anderson, *op. cit.*, see p. 278.

15. *Ibid.*, p. 291.

16. Gordon F. Streib, "Intergenerational Relations: Perspectives of the Two Generations on the Older Parent," *Journal of Marriage and the Family*, vol. 27 (November 1965), p. 472.

17. Clark and Anderson, *op. cit.*, p. 279.

18. Booth, *op. cit.*, p. 188. Booth defines the male associated activities as, "Instrumental associations, groups organized to cope with the external environment. . . ." The female associated activities he terms expressive which are organized

The Personal Dimension of Life Satisfaction 97

to prevent deviant behavior. "Their activities, basically accommodative and nurturant in character, include socialization and personality integration."

19. For discussion of this distinction see especially Andrew Billingsley, *Black Families in White America* (Englewood Cliffs, N.J.: Prentice-Hall, 1968), Chapter 1.

20. Frances M. Carp, "Retired People as Automobile Passengers," *Gerontologist,* vol. 12 (1972), pp. 66.

21. Francis L. K. Hsu, "American Core Value and National Character," in F. L. K. Hsu (ed.), *Psychological Anthropology: Approaches to Culture and Personality* Homewood, Ill.: Dorsey, 1961), pp. 218–19.

22. Margaret Clark, "Cultural Values and Dependency in Later Life," in Donald O. Cowgill and Lowell D. Holmes, *op. cit.,* p.273.

23. Our italics.

24. Thomas Tissue, "Another Look at Self-Rated Health Among the Elderly," *Journal of Gerontology,* vol. 27 (January 1974), p. 93.

25. This correlation is the part-whole correlation coefficient (Yule's Q) entailed in the Scalogram Analysis of the *Statistical Package for the Social Sciences.*

26. The complete CAPACITY index appears in Appendix B.

27. John N. Edwards and David L. Klemmack, "Correlates of Life Satisfaction: A Re-examination," *Journal of Gerontology,* vol. 28, no. 4 (1973), pp. 497-502, also point out some evidence contradictory to their hypothesis found in E. Palmore and C. Luikart, "Health and Social Factors Related to Life Satisfaction," *Journal of Health and Social Behavior* (1972), pp. 68–70. These authors find self-rated health to be the predominant variable accounting for satisfaction, and at the same time they find that socioeconomic factors are not significantly related to well-being. We have previously suggested that one's health is reciprocally related to one's sense of well-being.

28. Lopata, *op. cit.,* 54–55. Occasionally this relationship is dealt with rather extensively but within a very general theoretical context. For example, see Gubrium, *op. cit.*

29. Jaber F. Gubrium, "Apprehensions of Coping Incompetence and Responses to Fear in Old Age," *International Journal of Aging and Human Development,* vol. 4 (Spring 1973), pp. 117, 120.

30. See our discussion of felt competency on pp. 30-31, and our discussion of Lemon *et al.* on self-concept and life satisfaction on p. 70.

31. Clark, *op. cit.,* p. 264.

32. Irving Rosow, *Social Integration of the Aged* (New York: Free Press, 1967), p. 61.

33. See particularly Gordon F. Streib, "Old Age and the Family," *American*

Behavioral Scientist, vol. 14 (Spring 1970), p. 31; and Ethel Shanas, "Family Responsibility and the Health of Older People," *Journal of Gerontology,* vol. 15 (October 1960), p. 408.

34. Shanas, *ibid.,* pp. 408–11.

35. Robert S. Weiss, "The Fund of Sociability," in Helena Z. Lopata (ed.), *Marriages and Family* (New York: Van Nostrand, 1973), p. 200.

36. Streib, *op. cit.,* p. 31, notes that among people 65 years of age and older, 53 percent are married couples. Fifty-five percent of the people in our sample are married.

37. Paul Cameron, *et al.,* "Personality Differences Between Typical Urban Negroes and Whites," *Journal of Negro Education,* vol. 40 (1971), pp. 70, 72.

38. See Paul Cameron, *et al.,* "The Life Satisfaction of Nonnormal Persons," *Journal of Consulting and Clinical Psychology,* vol. 41, no. 2 (1973), p. 212.

39. E. g., logotherapists such as Victor Frankl, *The Doctor and the Soul* (New York: Alfred A. Knopf, 1962) and Elton D. Trueblood, *The Life We Prize* (New York: Harper and Brothers, 1951).

FIVE

The Environmental Dimension of Life Satisfaction

Introduction

Beyond the individual and his personal set of attributes and attitudes lies the environment. Because we interact with our environment, it can present us with opportunities for enhancing levels of morale or with stressful situations and barriers to obtaining a satisfying life. Because it has this potential for positively or negatively influencing our morale, environmental factors are of considerable importance to policy makers who affect the environment. Before we consider environmental influences on morale, we must arrive at an understanding of what we mean by "environment."

One way of defining the environment is to describe where it is found. It is difficult, if not impossible, to identify where self ends and the self's environment begins.[1] We are forced, therefore, to skirt this problem and to focus our attention on that space which clearly lies beyond the individual. Here we can divide the environment into two components dichotomized on the basis of spatial scale but predicated for the most part upon the degree of our concern with the environment.

The first and proximate environment extends from one's home to the boundary of a given residential neighborhood. This is the area of most immediate concern to us since we spend more time here than at any other place. In perceiving homes and neighborhoods as our own, our respective environments become a reflection of and on ourselves, if not indeed an extension of our personal identities. It is where most of the things labeled *ours* can be found. We shall call this portion of the environment simply the residential neighborhood. It is again difficult to identify the place where this portion of our environment ends and the next, more distant, commences; but each of us can identify an area about his home which is of direct concern in terms of acquaintances, safety, appearance and other residential attributes which we value.

The second and more distant portion of our environment includes everything beyond the immediate boundaries of the neighborhood. We will refer to this as the general urban environment. This portion of the environment is of less direct concern to each of us than is the neighborhood, except as we spend time in certain areas of it for specific purposes, such as shopping or visiting friends. It is here in the general urban environment that we find opportunities for obtaining the necessities as well as the amenities of life, e. g., places of employment, stores, banks, parks, etc.

Having defined portions of the environment which are of concern to us, we can now concentrate upon those elements of the environment which might be related to morale. This is a difficult task since so many environmental factors can be identified. For example, we hear a great deal today about the quality of our physical environment and certainly everyone desires a residential neighborhood which has clean air and low levels of visual and noise pollution. But do these physical elements actually affect our morale? Will cleaner air really make us happier? Even if we could precisely point to the fact that degradation of air quality is eroding our health and thereby indirectly influencing our morale, it would be nearly impossible to include in our study all the relevant variables that might be found in the physical, social, political and other environments. We have tried to include in the analysis all relevant environmental variables indicated by previous studies as well as additional variables which we believe are appropriate to the elderly and their special needs, including what the city can do for them. Thus, our set of environmental factors was initially limited to the variables selected for study and now devolves to those variables that are statistically significant components in a network of influences on life satisfaction.

The results of our analysis reveal three major networks of environmental factors which are related to life satisfaction. Two of the three networks fall within the neighborhood portion of the urban environment. The first focuses upon the density of elderly persons residing within a given geographical area and is referred to as a network of "Age Concentration." The second is called "Physical Security" because it revolves about two determinants of satisfaction, CONDITION OF NEIGHBORHOOD and INCOME ADEQUACY. The third network relates to the general urban environment and encompasses variables which reflect a person's level of mobility, specifically SELF-TRANSPORTATION, within that environment. Each of these networks is discussed in a separate section of this chapter. Before we turn to these sections, however, we should briefly consider how environmental influences on morale and our perceptions of the environment might vary with age.

Let us think of three types of household groupings representing different stages in the life cycle: a unit of young adults in the household formation stage; a family with school-age children; and finally a couple in their post-retirement years. All of these households reside within the same city and thus share the same general urban environment. However, each has elected to live in a different residential neighborhood. Within the constraints imposed upon them by their respective incomes and the capital they have been able to accumulate over the years, each has chosen the neighborhood and house or apartment most suited to his needs and desires. We can easily envision the young couple living in an older neighborhood, near the center of town, perhaps the same neighborhood as the older couple. In contrast, the middle-aged couple and their children reside in a typical suburban setting and have the usual suburban accouterments such as two cars, two TV sets, two bathrooms, etc.

Each of these hypothetical households is likely to view its neighborhood quite differently, even if all three were to reside in the same place. Let us consider the case of possible neighborhood decline. The younger couple is apt to have little concern about the gradually declining quality of their neighborhood since they don't envision a protracted residence there. The middle-aged couple is quite concerned about any decline since they are investing in the neighborhood by purchasing their house and perhaps by adding improvements. They don't anticipate living there forever, but do not know how long it will be before they can construct their ideal home. They know, however, that if the quality of the neighborhood declines, their investment will shrink and they might never obtain that new home and its attendant status. The oldest couple is probably most concerned. This neighborhood is "theirs" and has been for perhaps several decades. This is where they have invested many years and where they expect to remain.

Similar variations in the amount of concern generated over other less tangible changes in the perceived quality of the neighborhood also can be easily imagined. For example, a perceived negative change in the socioeconomic composition of the neighborhood, perhaps induced by the influx of a particular minority group, would be least troublesome to the younger couple who are the most likely of the three families to be sympathetic to the notion of ethnic or racial integration. It is also quite likely that they do not spend as much time neighboring as do their older counterparts since much of their leisure time is spent in activities outside the neighborhood. The couple with children, however, would be very much concerned not only about their financial investment but about the quality of schools and the social relationships their children will establish within the neighborhood. The older couple, whose values were conditioned in an era when general racial and/or ethnic strife seldom received great attention but who have been puzzled by its recent explosive manifestations, are perhaps even more troubled than the others. They feel deeply involved in their neighborhood. Most of their social network is probably found there and certainly some very old acquaintances. It is the older couple who witness the departure of old neighbors and who must think of spending the rest of their lives with "the new people" since the likelihood of their relocating to another neighborhood is very slight.

It is relatively easy to extend such generalizations to the greater urban environment as well. Nearly everyone moves about the city transacting personal business or undertaking other activities such as shopping, working, visiting friends and going to school. Prior research reveals that the levels of such activity within the general urban environment decline over the life span, particularly after retirement. A recent Harris study, for example, shows that a national sample of persons age 65 and over reported lower attendance by aged persons at many kinds of activities ranging from shopping to going to a public park.[2] Older persons reported generally higher levels of attendance than the remainder of the population only at church or synagogue. This general decline in activity and trip frequency has been noted in several other studies as well.[3]

Moreover, we find that the relative importance and frequency of specific activities and their attendant trips change with increased age. For the general population, travel outside the neighborhood to school is later replaced by work trips. Upon retirement, total trip frequency declines as daily work trips are no longer undertaken, but slight increases are often reported in shopping and other types of trips. Contrary to Carp's suggestion, the social trip is not underrepresented among the elderly, but is generally made in somewhat greater proportion by older persons.[4]

Thus we find that over the life span, interaction with the general urban environment changes both in nature and frequency of contact. Certain life support activities such as shopping and personal business transactions remain fairly stable; others, school or work for example, remain constant for long periods of time; while still others, such as social and recreational activities, fluctuate widely from one life cycle stage to another. With declines in activity levels, researchers note concomitant lowering levels of awareness of the general urban environment and the activity opportunities it offers.[5] Explanations for these changes through time in an individual's relation to the general urban environment range from simple and obvious (e. g., retirement and decline in work trips) to highly complex and multi-faceted (e. g., lowering levels of awareness as to what the general urban environment contains).

The context, then, in which we present the remainder of our results is one of urban environments which extend beyond the individual to the neighborhood and beyond that to the general urban environment. In many ways, the relationships which exist among older people and these urban environments are similar to those of other age cohorts. There are, however, subtle and important differences, especially as the environment impacts upon the older person. Some of these differences become immediately apparent when we examine the relationships between age-homogeneous neighborhoods and life satisfaction.

The Age Concentration Network
and the Neighborhood Environment

The importance of the social environment to the morale of the aged is well established in previous studies.[6] Much of this work has focused upon variations in social interaction and friendship networks which are found in different living environments. Although such studies generally consider very small neighborhood units, e.g., dwelling units within an apartment complex, it is generally concluded that age homogeneity, propinquity, common socioeconomic status and similarity of values and interests facilitate high levels of social interaction and friendship formation.[7] The majority of these studies focus upon the simple dichotomous situation of age homogeneity/heterogeneity. Obviously age homogeneity implies some form of segregation or exclusionary practice. Although such a dichotomy facilitates analysis, it is difficult to enumerate many situations in which this occurs in any strict sense. Age homogeneity does occur in special housing projects and retirement communities, but the majority of urban elderly do not reside in such settings; most live in social and physical environments popularly defined as neighborhoods.

Although few studies of the urban elderly have addressed social interaction and the establishment of friendship networks across a wide range of neighborhoods, it is reasonable to expect the same factors which have been shown to be influential in age homogeneous/heterogeneous studies to be operating in a broader spatial context.[8] It is logical to believe that the nature of socio-environmental influences are more continuous than discrete. Thus, our study utilizes variables of age concentration rather than age homogeneity.

Several measures of age concentration were considered. Each was derived from the number of persons age 62 and older residing in those census tracts reported for the study area in 1970. The first measure considered was the density of elderly persons per dwelling unit. Another measure of the concentration of elderly people was the calculation of the elderly population density per square mile of land encompassed within the census tract. The third measure was simply the percent of the population in each tract that was elderly. Simple correlation analysis revealed strong positive relationships among all three measures (for example, r = .99 for % ELDERLY and the density per square mile). Additional examination showed that each of the density measures reported lowest concentrations in the same suburban tracts and high values in tracts near the Central Business District. Because of the apparent redundancy among these measures, the most easily intelligible, % ELDERLY, was selected as the measure of age concentration. In addition, because of this variable's close association with the square mile density variable, we also can deduce that elderly residents of tracts with high concentrations also experience close spatial proximity to other elderly people. This variable is found to be significantly related to MORALE (beta = .09), and also forms the focus of a network of variables which indirectly influence MORALE, Figure 5.1 The analysis reveals a positive relationship leading from the age concentration variable, % ELDERLY, to MORALE, indicating that

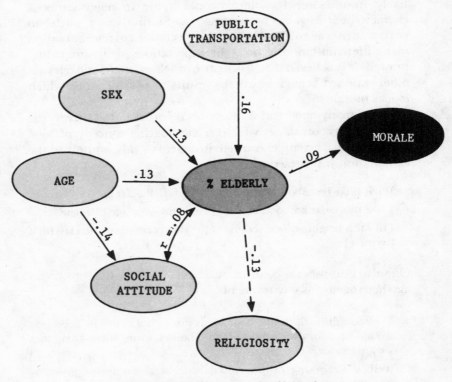

Figure 5.1 Age Concentration Network

elderly people residing in neighborhoods with high concentrations of older residents have higher levels of life satisfaction.

In Chapter 2, we noted that age homogeneity/heterogeneity of the social environment influences life satisfaction, although there is conflicting evidence as to whether the relationship is positive or negative. Our study indicates that the relationship is a positive one. Interpretation of this relationship rests upon two related explanations: (1) the burdensome nature of the broad spectrum of activities that arises in age-heterogeneous environments; and (2) the concept of role consonance/dissonance. The former states that elderly people residing in age-heterogeneous environments face a maximum variety of social and activity situations and that the older person's ease in performing one activity may not mean similar ease in other activities. The potential frustration and psychic conflict resulting from this inability to perform is very likely troublesome for older people living in neighborhoods characterized as age heterogeneous. Similarly, in such an environment the role and behavior expectations of relevant others may differ substantially from the expectations of the individual himself. It is believed that dissonance in self-expected and relevant other-expected behavior patterns results in psychic stress which erodes morale.[9]

Of the many open-ended responses reported in the survey, the vast majority of those which relate to the concept of age-homogeneous/heterogeneous environments lends support to the explanation just presented.

> What I like best about my neighborhood is that older people live here.
>
> I like this neighborhood because people my own age live here.
>
> I like this neighborhood because of the elderly people of our class [that live here].

One also glimpses the conflict and stress which are likely to attend age-heterogeneous environments.

> The most difficult thing about life is just trying to live it. Teenagers around here are always breaking into houses, using dope. Their dogs are a nuisance.
>
> Well, if the young people would leave us alone, we might enjoy something.

I don't like anything about this neighborhood. I do like my apartment though. The worst thing about the neighborhood is all these destructive kids that live around here. They steal gas, use BB guns on windows.

The best thing for an older person to do is to stay out of younger people's way.

The latter comments strongly suggest that stress can be a more open and direct result of age-heterogeneous neighborhoods than simply the suble discomfort engendered by role consonance/ dissonance. Whatever the specific contributing factors might be, we conclude that morale tends to be higher among older people in socio-environments where aged persons are relatively prevalent. Conversely, neighborhoods of age heterogeneity where elderly people are likely to be a minority tend to be deleterious to high levels of life satisfaction.

The network of relationships leading to and from the age concentration variable, % ELDERLY, is shown in Figure 5.1 Elderly people residing in neighborhoods near the city's center, which have high concentrations of elderly people and disproportionate numbers of females and older elderly persons, are more apt to use public transportation and to have a higher SOCIAL ATTITUDE than persons residing in neighborhoods with lower densities of elderly residents. These neighborhoods of high concentration would be characterized as older and generally stable residential portions of the city.

Figure 5.1 further reveals that the density of elderly residents is significantly related to an individual's utilization of public transportation (a link in the network showing a .16 beta leading from PUBLIC TRANSPORTATION to % ELDERLY). Public transportation in this case is fixed-route bus transit service. The direction of the relationship suggests that public transit induces concentrations of elderly persons. Although it is likely that a few elderly people relocating their residence within the city might choose to reside in an area where public transit is available, we generally find that transit service because of its "profit" orientation is found in older urban areas with high population densities and particularly in neighborhoods with heavy concentrations of those considered to be "transit dependent," i.e., those who do not have automobiles available to them. It is not surprising, then, that a simple analysis comparing % ELDERLY between transit users and those reporting no transit use shows a marked and significant (P<.01) difference in elderly densities of 17.5 and 14.7 percent respectively. Obviously in places where transit exists and elderly persons use it, we find neighborhoods of high elderly population density. This does not mean, however, that most or even many of the people in our sample are well served by public transit even though many of them reside in neighborhoods of high elderly population density. Only 12 percent of our sample reported transit use despite the fact that 52 percent do not own an automobile. .

The variables SEX and AGE are also positively related to concentrations of aged persons; each has a beta of .13 leading from it to % ELDERLY. To help clarify the exact nature of these relationships, Table 5.1 is developed showing a breakdown of % ELDERLY by AGE and SEX. Dividing the sample into three age groupings results in a significant and positive progression in elderly density from the lowest to highest ages. This relationship holds among females in the sample but to a lesser extent among the males. Males at all ages report lower neighborhood densities of older people while females are disproportionately found in higher density neighborhoods. Thus, we find that both older people and females tend to reside in neighborhoods which have higher densities of older people.

Residents of neighborhoods having higher concentrations of elderly persons not only tend to be older, more likely to be female and to use public transit, but they also report lower levels of FAMILY DEPENDENCE. The relationships leading to DEPENDENCE ON FAMILY also have been considered in Chapter 4 (pp. 88-95). It is sufficient to note that those who are most dependent on relatives appear to be women and older elderly people of both sexes. It is worth reiterating that, even though neighborhoods with high concentrations of aging persons have disproportionate shares of women and older elderly, the people in these neighborhoods are still generally less dependent upon their relatives.

Table 5.2 demonstrates this point by comparing the average reported elderly population concentrations for those who are and are not family dependent, while controlling for differences in AGE and SEX. As we have pointed out, males and younger elderly tend to reside in neighborhoods with lower concentrations of elderly

Table 5.1   Census Tract Concentration of Elderly by Age and Sex

Characteristics	Average Percent Elderly Within Census Tracts
Age*	
60–69 years of age	14.09
70–79 years	14.93
80+ years	16.21
Sex* and Age	
Male	14.04
60–69	13.39
70–79	12.72
80+	16.08
Female	15.66
60–69	14.69
70–79	15.96
80+	16.45

*Significant difference at 0.05 level of confidence when tested via ANOVA.

Table 5.2   Census Tract Concentration of Elderly
Controlling for Family Dependence

Characteristic	Average Percent Elderly	
	Family Dependent	Not Family Dependent
Males	13.65	14.29
Females	14.66	16.73
Age 60–69	13.51	14.60
Age 70–79	14.11	15.47
Age 80+	15.22	17.20
Total Sample	14.24	15.76

people than do women and very old people. Given this situation, we find that for both sexes and all age groups those who report dependence on family reside in neighborhoods which have lower densities of elderly residents. Thus, we conclude that older people residing in neighborhoods with high concentrations of elderly persons are slightly less dependent on others in general, despite the fact that such neighborhoods have disproportionate shares of older elderly persons and elderly women—two groups having higher dependency rates. Moreover, to the extent that dependency is found in such neighborhoods, it tends to be oriented toward friends and neighbors (presumably elderly ones) as opposed to relatives.

Concomitant with lower dependence on family members and compensatory reliance on other elderly is a heightened SOCIAL ATTITUDE for residents of neighborhoods with high elderly population densities (Fig. 5.1). This scaled measure of expressed desire to see more of friends, relatives, and neighbors and a preference for eating meals with others is positively correlated with the density of older people. The nature of this relationship is shown to be reciprocal, indicating that the more gregarious tend to be concentrated in neighborhoods with a high concentration of elderly people; and that residing and socializing in such a setting can reinforce positive attitudes towards social contact. It should also be remembered that SOCIAL ATTITUDE is itself an intervening variable leading positively to ACTIVITY, i.e., people in these neighborhoods not only have higher levels of SOCIAL ATTITUDE but also behaviorally express it with higher levels of ACTIVITY.

AGE is negatively related to SOCIAL ATTITUDE. This in itself is not surprising since increased age is often accompanied by loss of friends and social contacts, declining health, and lower mobility. However, the fact that neighborhoods with high concentrations of older persons have disproportionate numbers of older elderly people and still report higher SOCIAL ATTITUDE is noteworthy. Again, as is the case with family dependence, the conclusion is suggested that positive social effects continue to accrue to older residents of age-concentrated neighborhoods long after such effects have begun to atrophy for those elderly who reside in more heterogeneous environments.

These findings can also be interpreted in light of continuity and other theories of life satisfaction. It would appear that for many elderly people, the desire to socialize remains fairly high, perhaps declining with health rather than simply age. If, as our data show, those elderly persons who reside in neighborhoods of high elderly concentration interact more with friends and neighbors and have a higher SOCIAL ATTITUDE, then higher interaction quite likely results from the greater opportunity these people have for interacting with peers. Elderly people living in more isolated social environments might report lower SOCIAL ATTITUDE because they lack opportunities for peer interaction or because they have adjusted to their isolation by reducing expressed desire for social contacts. As we have already noted, social interaction in age-heterogeneous social settings is more difficult and apt to be more stressful than in age-homogeneous environments.

This interpretation which emphasizes social integration versus social isolation is reinforced when we consider the relationship between RELIGIOSITY and % ELDERLY. Although one might assume that religiosity is an intellectual or psychological derivative, rather than a socio-environmental factor, our analysis indicates that religiosity might be derived also from the social environment. At least, socio-environmental factors may intensify or reinforce religiosity. Thus, we present a brief examination of the network of interrelationships which focuses upon RELIGIOSITY.

The Religiosity Network

We would not expect religious belief to be an important part of the life of every member of society, and therefore of our sample. At the same time, religious belief is important in every known society, and we therefore would expect it to be important to the lives of a portion of the people in our sample. The question for us is how does having a religious belief relate to other aspects of an older person's life, particularly those aspects that in turn affect life satisfaction? There is a widespread notion that religious conviction becomes stronger as death becomes more probable. If this is true, then religiosity is an important aspect of personal experience in old age.

In constructing our measure of religious belief, RELIGIOSITY, we were mindful of the predominant religious background of the people who constitute the community from which our sample is drawn, which is conventional Christianity. Thus, the religious beliefs of our respondents (those who are religious) in almost all cases would be conventionally Christian. Accordingly, for our measure, RELIGIOSITY is represented by a belief in an after-life. A person's RELIGIOSITY score is determined by whether or not such a belief is present and how emphatic it is.

Respondents were asked to complete the following statement,

"When a person dies, he . . . ." There turned out to be basically three categories of responses to this open-ended question. One category consists of essentially secular responses; for example, "He dies." "Everything is finished." "He's just dead, that's all." "He just dies." The second consists of responses that express socially acceptable religious conventions without revealing much personal feeling; for instance, "Goes on to a better life." "Goes to Heaven." "I suppose he goes to his reward." "Has passed on out of this world." "He goes to one of two places." "Goes to the hereafter." The final category reveals strong personal convictions about the existence of an after-life, its substance, and the terms on which individuals are related to it; for example, "There is a Heaven and Hell and God will take care of the good people that served him." "I want to go to Heaven. Everyone should live so that they can go to Heaven and be with the Lord." "Is gone to the greatest reward there is if he has so lived a Christian life where he is really prepared." "I believe in the Lord, in the hereafter, and a Heaven where I hope I will go when I die."

The actual network of relationships leading to RELIGIOSITY is composed of many elements, Figure 5.2. As was already indicated, a strong negative relationship exists between the age concentration variable % ELDERLY and RELIGIOSITY, indicating that those residing in neighborhoods with low proportions of elderly residents are more apt to express strong feelings of religious sentiment. From the other relationships in this network we can characterize these people as being white widows or widowers, with relatively low incomes (although those with spouses have higher incomes), but high levels of ACTIVITY and AUTO OWNERSHIP. Despite their low income status, they report strong positive levels of INCOME ADEQUACY. From the spatial distribution of % ELDERLY we can deduce that these people generally reside in less central and somewhat more suburban neighborhoods of the city. This is also in keeping with the RACE relationship which indicates that blacks who reside almost exclusively in the inner city ghetto with high population density do not report such high levels of religious commitment.

Given the negative relationships between being married and RELIGIOSITY and between peer concentration and RELIGIOSITY, we suggest that the extent of one's religious belief tends to increase

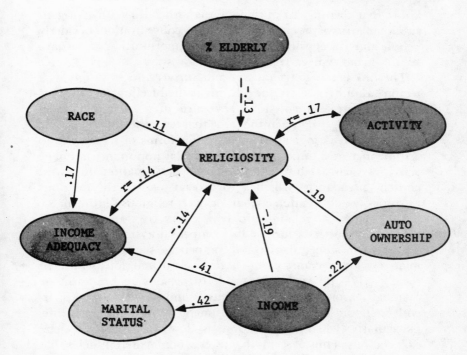

Figure 5.2 Religiosity Network.

with social isolation. However, there are also complex relationships embodied within this network. As a case in point, INCOME
appears to be a focal point for several of these complex
relationships. To begin with, INCOME is negatively related to
RELIGIOSITY, suggesting that religious belief may compensate for
economic deprivation. INCOME relates positively to MARITAL STATUS
(being married) since both spouses provide some portion of the
fixed income. The negative relationship between MARITAL STATUS
and RELIGIOSITY again reinforces the compensatory nature of
RELIGIOSITY: that is, religious belief may compensate for loss of
companionship (compounded by loss in income).[10] Furthermore,
INCOME impacts positively on AUTO OWNERSHIP for obvious
reasons. The positive relationship of AUTO OWNERSHIP on
RELIGIOSITY obliquely reveals another form of deprivation,
environmental isolation. We offer this interpretation because we

know that owning an automobile is associated with living in suburban areas of the city which have low concentrations of elderly people and low densities of all activity opportunities. As we have seen, % ELDERLY negatively affects RELIGIOSITY.

The link between RELIGIOSITY and ACTIVITY, interestingly, is a reciprocal one. If, as we suggest, intensified feelings of religious sentiment are influenced by residence in a socially isolated neighborhood, isolated in the sense that few other elderly people are nearby, it is logical to expect other forms of socializing to assume increased importance. Of particular importance might be activities such as clubs and/or church participation. Increased church attendance, whether for social or strictly religious purposes, would reinforce latent or overt religious sentiment.

The reciprocal relationship between INCOME ADEQUACY and RELIGIOSITY suggests further the compensatory role of religious sentiment in an acquisitive and competitive society. Those with relatively low incomes report high levels of religious sentiment (beta = -.17); however, these elderly persons report adequate material resources to meet their needs and expectations. Apparently religious belief fosters adjustment to one's station in life, particularly when that station is low relative to societal expectations. Thus, it seems that those whom material success has eluded transfer their aspirations from this life to "the next."

In summary, the foregoing analysis has focused upon age concentration, which is an intervening variable in one of the paths leading to life satisfaction. Neighborhoods with high concentrations of aging persons provide an environment conducive to high levels of social interaction and encourage positive attitudes toward social contact. This finding supports previous research that age-homogeneous environments are less stressful and facilitate positive social interactions.

Our analysis goes further in revealing the salutary effects such environments have on morale. For example, most of these neighborhoods are in the older areas of the city and their age composition results from aging-in-place rather than deliberate migrations or residential relocations. As a consequence, these areas have disproportionate concentrations of older elderly persons and elderly females. Despite the fact that such persons normally tend to be more dependent on others, especially relatives, we find dependency levels lower than in other areas of the city. In place of dependency on relatives, there is reliance on peers, friends and neighbors. It is likely that reliance on others who share similar problems is preferable to being a "burden on the family." Additional freedom from being a burden on others—not just family—accrues from another salutary aspect of age-concentrated neighborhoods, i.e., mass transit. Mass transit, when it exists, allows elderly people to "get about" without being dependent on others for their transportation needs.

Moreover, we see that people residing in socially isolated physical settings, i.e., neighborhoods with few older people, offset this isolation by greater participation in organized group activities, particularly church activities. Such older people express stronger religious sentiments than do residents of less isolated environments.

All of these findings demonstrate that the neighborhood environment is strongly related to levels of MORALE within the general urban population of elderly residents. Such findings are significant in an applied sense when we recognize that most public policy decisions at the local level, especially those undertaken by urban planners and others, directly affect neighborhood environments. In our presentation of the next network of path relations leading to MORALE, the importance of the neighborhood environment is reinforced.

The Physical Security Network

Physical security and all that this concept encompasses have long been thought to be related to the morale of older people. Prior research identifies two major and interrelated dimensions of physical security: financial circumstances and the quality of the neighborhood environment. The relationships between these dimensions and morale have been noted in several studies. Kutner, for example, finds that income is positively related to morale, although he concludes that employment has a greater impact than does income in and of itself.[11] Spreitzer and Snyder demonstrate that financial status is an important predictor of life satisfaction; however, they conclude that perceived financial adequacy is a stronger predictor than more objective indicators.[12] Edwards and Klemmack show that socioeconomic status, particularly income, is strongly related to morale.[13] They also conclude that neighboring is very important. Clark and Anderson reinforce these findings by indicating that the sources of high morale include, among other things, physical comforts and physical security.[14]

The two dimensions of physical security—financial circumstances and neighborhood quality—are generally assumed to be interrelated since social research on the general urban population reveals that household socioeconomic status, particularly income, is strongly related to the judged quality of neighborhood environments. There is reason to suspect that this relationship is less true for urban elderly residents, however, since they are relatively less mobile residentially and are often found in neighborhoods which have undergone considerable change, usually decline.

In operationalizing the theoretical model of life satisfaction, the concept of physical security was measured by income-related variables and measures of perceived neighborhood quality. It was expected that the variables of income and neighborhood quality would be closely related and would jointly constitute a dimension reflecting a condition of perceived physical security. Simple regression analysis reveals a significant but slight correlation between the variable CONDITION OF NEIGHBORHOOD and INCOME, as well as between CONDITION OF NEIGHBORHOOD and INCOME ADEQUACY, $r = .23$ and $r = .22$ respectively. There also exist comparably weak correlations between CONDITION OF NEIGHBORHOOD and CAPACITY, MEDICAL and RACE. In the path analysis with MORALE, however, we find no significant relationship between the neighborhood quality measure and the income variables, indicating that these are two fairly distinct dimensions of physical security, Figure 5.3. The variable CONDITION OF NEIGHBORHOOD is essentially a scaled measure of judged attractiveness and safety, and the income variables measure the size of annual income and the adequacy of that income as judged by the respondent. Because the two dimensions are unrelated in the path analysis, we will consider them separately.

CONDITION OF NEIGHBORHOOD as judged by the respondents is generally quite good. Twenty-five percent rated their neighbor-

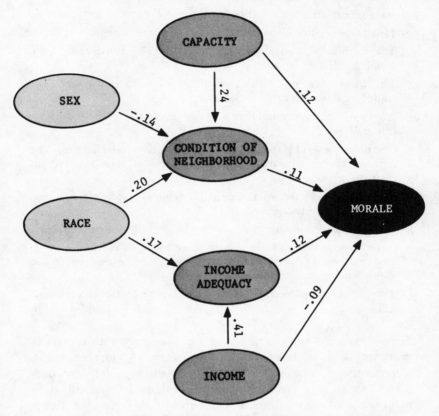

Figure 5.3 Physical Security Network

hoods very high and 44 percent thought their neighborhoods were above average. Another 21 percent had some reservations as to neighborhood quality, and 11 percent rated their local environments as very poor in terms of both safety and attractiveness. Not surprisingly, persons in the latter group reside primarily in inner city neighborhoods which would be characterized as transitional, unstable or even blighted. The following typical open-ended responses illustrate specific neighborhood qualities.

It's fairly quiet around here. I love my own privacy.

No one bothers you around here.

It's a nice quiet white neighborhood.

This place is convenient to the grocery store and the doctor's.

The neighborhood is convenient for stores and a bus stop is close. Some people don't keep up their property.

This neighborhood is quiet, [but] the city won't clean it up. [They could] move some of this junk out.

All these duplexes around here now and the renters are careless about things.

The neighborhood is running down. Houses need to be fixed up. The city could keep weeds out. Senior citizens should be helped to fix up their property.

There are a lot of shady characters in this neighborhood. Senior citizens should get more protection.

People are nice and respect my age [but] I don't like the bad teenagers.

[After a recent move,] I like this neighborhood—its so much quieter. The city should protect older people from crime. I've been robbed and another house was torn up.

The city should prosecute these youngsters who break in and rob old folks.

From comments such as these, we see that safety with respect to property is a significant concern for many elderly people. Neighborhood appearance is also important, especially to home owners with a continuing and long-term interest in their neighborhood. Conditions of quiet and privacy are also highly valued. In addition, changing racial and age composition, as well as changes in tenure, are a source of anxiety for elderly persons who testify to a perceived decline in the quality of their neighborhoods. Thus, the criteria by which older persons judge the condition of their neighborhoods encompasses more than attractiveness and safety, although these are two key elements.

CONDITION OF NEIGHBORHOOD is found to be positively related to MORALE in the path analysis, beta = .11. Obviously better neighborhood conditions relate to higher levels of morale. Negative neighborhood qualities contribute to feelings of anxiety, stress and fear and appear to be detrimental to morale, since respondents living in such environments report significantly lower levels of life satisfaction.

CONDITION OF NEIGHBORHOOD is also an intervening variable between MORALE and the variables of CAPACITY and SEX. CAPACITY is directly related to MORALE and, as the focal point of a network of relationships leading to MORALE, it was discussed in Chapter 4. The relationship here to CONDITION OF NEIGHBORHOOD, however, deserves some elaboration. A positive influence, beta = .24, leading from CAPACITY to CONDITION OF NEIGHBORHOOD reveals that those who are better able to perform daily tasks judge their neighborhoods to be of higher quality than those who are less capable. Recall that those people reporting lower CAPACITY are generally older, living alone, and have more frequent medical problems. Such people feel most threatened in an environment with actual or perceived high crime rates, since they are incapable of defending themselves or their property. It is also reasonable to postulate that those people with higher physical capacity are able and likely to spend a considerable amount of time and effort in "keeping up" their property. This might well contribute to a sense of satisfaction with self and with a neighborhood to which they are making a positive contribution.

SEX is found to be negatively related to CONDITION OF NEIGHBORHOOD; that is, there is a tendency for women to live in poorer neighborhoods. As was pointed out in the preceding section of this chapter, older elderly people in general and elderly women in particular are more heavily concentrated in the city's older neighborhoods—those neighborhoods which are often in a state of transition and/or decline. This is primarily caused by high levels of home ownership and resultant inertia with respect to change in residence which constitutes aging-in-place. As household members age within a neighborhood, males, because of higher death rates at lower ages, are survived by widows who increasingly constitute the elderly cohort of an older neighborhood's population. Since it is these older neighborhoods which are generally perceived to be of lower quality and since women comprise a significant proportion of the residents in these areas, it is to be expected that women as opposed to men more frequently report a negative assessment of neighborhood quality.

The positive relationship between RACE and CONDITION OF NEIGHBORHOOD reflects another aspect of the situation described above. Blacks judge their neighborhoods to be of lower quality than do whites. Again, the explanation is clear. Blacks reside almost exclusively in the oldest inner city areas where neighborhoods are less safe and less attractive. Many elderly whites share this condition, but many also are found in better quality neighborhoods scattered throughout the city. Even though all old people are geographically constrained by the vicissitudes of age, blacks are further constrained by racial discrimination.

We find, then, that the neighborhood dimension of physical security is directly related to MORALE. We also find that other factors such as SEX, RACE and CAPACITY are related to this dimension: blacks, women and elderly people with low CAPACITY are more likely to judge neighborhood quality as low and also report lower MORALE. Not surprisingly, we find cases of strongest neighborhood-related low MORALE in older, inner-city neighborhoods where the environment is physically declining and crime rates are high or rising.

Somewhat surprising, however, is the lack of interrelation between the neighborhood dimension and the fiscal dimension. The obvious expectation that people with higher incomes would reside in better quality neighborhoods cannot be substantiated for elderly persons in this study. We find many elderly persons with relatively high incomes, high in comparison to other elderly people, residing in some of the poorest quality neighborhoods. The most likely explanation is due to aging-in-place, i.e., the residential stability of older people in neighborhoods which are now unstable and in a period of decline. Because elderly persons relocate their residences most infrequently (average duration of residence in our sample approaches 30 years at the same location), it is logical to expect that these people closely fit the socioeconomic profile of their neighborhoods when they first located there many years ago. Over the years, although their relative status did not change, their neighborhood underwent considerable change in socioeconomic character. Thus, we find considerable discrepancies between the socioeconomic status (particularly INCOME) of elderly persons and that of their neighborhoods. Consequently, there exists no relationship between the two dimensions of physical security, financial status and quality of neighborhood.

We now turn to the other major dimension of physical security, which reflects financial circumstances and includes the variables

INCOME and INCOME ADEQUACY. Because of the persistent emphasis given to income by social scientists and policy makers, we pay particular attention to this variable in the interpretation of our findings.

The distribution of annual income within our sample is shown in Table 5.3. The range of incomes is wide, from a low of $600 to a high of $22,000. Slightly more than one quarter of the sample reports annual income of less than $2,000, while more than one half receives income of less than $5,000. Mean annual income is $4,280 with a standard deviation of $3,462, which means that the distribution is skewed relatively low in terms of range but is widely dispersed.

The median income of our sample ($3,306) is virtually the same as the national median income for household heads age 60 and over in owner occupied housing units ($3,300).[15] This comparison is appropriate since 81 percent of our sample own their own homes (and of these, only 10 percent are still making mortgage payments). The proportion of elderly homeowners nationally is 69 percent. Therefore, the level of income in our sample is comparable to older homeowners elsewhere, but the proportion of homeowners in our sample is somewhat greater than it is nationally.

Table 5.3   Sample Income Distribution (N=463)

Annual Income Group ($)	Percent of Sample
600 – 999	3
1,000 – 1,999	23
2,000 – 2,999	16
3,000 – 3,999	16
4,000 – 4,999	15
5,000 – 5,999	6
6,000 – 6,999	5
7,000 – 7,999	4
8,000 – 8,999	4
9,000 – 22,000	6

Mean $4,279.85
Median $3,306.00

The results of a stepwise multiple regression analysis, entering the dependent variable INCOME with all other variables in our study, are shown in Table 5.4. The equation explains 46 percent of the variance within the INCOME variable. It reflects first the strong positive relationship between INCOME and INCOME ADEQUACY. More will be said of this relationship shortly. The second variable in the equation is AUTO OWNERSHIP which has a strong simple correlation coefficient with INCOME, r = .48. Obviously, auto owners among elderly people in our sample are wealthier than those not owning automobiles.

Table 5.4   Regression Analysis with INCOME the Dependent Variable*

Independent Variable	B	R	R^2	r
Income Adequacy	.30	.50	.25	.50
Auto Ownership	.20	.56	.35	.48
Age	.15	.62	.39	-.33
Marital Status	.19	.64	.42	.42
Employment Status	.15	.67	.44	.28
Education	.15	.68	.46	.25

*Additional significant variables contribute less than 1 percent to variance explained and are therefore deleted.

AGE is an important correlate of INCOME and is found to be negatively related, r = -.33. Older elderly persons report significantly lower incomes as is shown in Table 5.5. There appears to be slightly more than a decline of $1,000 in mean annual income with each increasing decade of age. This is due to many reasons such as declining pension funds, insurance benefits and interest earned on savings, as well as a decline in the level of MARITAL STATUS. The number of people with spouses declines with increasing age due to increasingly high death rates. MARITAL STATUS, being married, is positively related to INCOME, r = .42, as is EMPLOYMENT status, r = .28, and EDUCATION, r = .25. The variables which constitute this equation are those which researchers have reported for the general population as well as the elderly. A possible exception is AUTO OWNERSHIP, which is seldom found for the general population but which is noted repeatedly for the elderly cohort.[16]

Table 5.5   Distribution of Mean Annual Income
by Age, Race, and Income Adequacy Group

Variable/Group	Mean Annual Income	Number of Observations
Age 60–69	$5,537.43	171
70–79	4,114.77	142
80+	3,002.48	150
Race		
Whites	3,094.54	343
Blacks	3,649.95	97
Income Adequacy		
Inadequate	2,299.18	96
Just Adequate	3,678.24	238
More than Adequate	7,115.35	119

The conclusion that must be drawn from the foregoing analyses is that the income distribution of our sample and the socio-economic factors correlating with INCOME conform to expectations based on previous research. This basic consistency with the findings of others should be kept in mind as we elaborate on the path model of physical security.

In Figure 5.3 income size impacts on the adequacy of one's income with a beta of .41. This indicates that higher income frequently results in higher reported INCOME ADEQUACY. However, we find many cases that do not conform to these expectations. Table 5.6 shows that the great majority of people in the "inadequate" category report low levels of income, and a majority of those in the "more than adequate" category have high levels of income. However, about one quarter of the "more than adequate" group is found at the lowest income levels. Further, a majority of the people in the "adequate" group report the lowest level of income.

It should be recalled that INCOME ADEQUACY is included in the analysis as well as income size because it reflects in part an additional dimension of physical security. We have found cases of people with very low incomes who report adequate or more than

Table 5.6   Relation of INCOME Size to INCOME ADEQUACY

	Income is Inadequate	Income is Adequate	Income is more than Adequate
Below Mean Income Group (0 – $3,999)	90	174	36
Mean Income Group ($4,000 – $5,999)	8	55	33
Above Mean Income Group ($6,000+)	2	30	64
Total in Group	100	259	133

adequate income, and opposite cases as well. The question from which the measure is derived (see p. 40) was designed to reflect as accurately as possible the extent to which people's incomes actually covered their expenses during a given period. So we feel it elicits a somewhat different dimension of financial condition from measures of "satisfaction with one's income," such as that used by Spreitzer and Snyder.[17] However, it will reflect differences in the extent of people's needs and their expectations.

Figure 5.3 indicates not only that INCOME and INCOME ADEQUACY are related, but that both of these variables impact directly on MORALE. In Table 5.7 we see that most of the "inadequate income" group falls in the "low morale" category, while the "adequate income" group is almost evenly distributed between "low" and "high morale," and most of the "more than adequate income" group falls in the "high morale" category, as would be expected.

On the other hand, a conceptual problem arises from the direct and *negative* influence of INCOME on MORALE (see Fig. 5.3). The negative finding is the result of INCOME's influence on MORALE when the other variables in the regression equation are held constant, particularly INCOME ADEQUACY. (The zero-order correlation between INCOME and MORALE is a positive .17.) The key to this paradox is to be found in the influence of INCOME on MORALE when INCOME ADEQUACY is held constant. The complex relationship among these three variables is depicted in Table 5.7. The mean income of our entire sample falls within the $4,000 to $5,999 category. If we assume that all respondents with below average income should fall in the "low morale" category, and all with above average income in the "high morale" category, then we can consider respondents who do not meet these expectations as representing error in the INCOME-MORALE relationship, controlling for INCOME ADEQUACY. The bracketed figures in Table 5.7, then, signify errors. It can be seen that there is virtually the same proportion of errors in the "below average" income categories as in the "above average" income categories (note "Totals" column), which is another indication that it is the intervention of INCOME ADEQUACY that matters. There is a steady progression in the proportion of errors from the "inadequate" group (29 percent) to the "more than adequate" group (38 percent). The least deviation from theoretical expectations, therefore, is in the former group and the greatest deviation is in the latter group.

Further concentrated research on this subject is necessary before the interrelated findings we have presented here can be fully explained. However, given our evidence, we would hypothesize

Table 5.7   The relationship Among INCOME, INCOME ADEQUACY, and MORALE

INCOME Group	Inadequate INCOME		Adequate INCOME		More than Adequate INCOME		Totals
	LOW MORALE	HIGH MORALE	LOW MORALE	HIGH MORALE	LOW MORALE	HIGH MORALE	
0 - $1,999	42	[15]	44	[33]	6	[15]	N=300
$2,000 - 3,999	20	[13]	55	[42]	5	[10]	E=128 %E=43
4,000 - 5,999	5	3	25	30	14	19	
6,000 - 7,999	[1]	1	[4]	11	[10]	16	
8,000 - 9,999	--	--	[3]	3	[4]	7	
10,000 - 11,999	--	--	[3]	1	[6]	3	N=96
12,000 - 13,999	--	--	[1]	2	[3]	5	E=39
14,000 - 15,999	--	--	--	--	--	3	%E=41
16,000 - 17,999	--	--	[1]	--	[1]	3	
18,000+	--	--	[1]	--	[1]	2	
N	100		259		133		
Error	29		88		50		
% Error	29		34		38		

that the explanation for INCOME's negative impact on MORALE is that in enough cases, older people with relatively high incomes have experienced traumatic reductions in income size relative to their younger years, while a sufficient number of people who have been relatively poor all their adult lives do not experience substantial financial discontinuity. An illustration of this phenomenon would be a comparison between a person whose annual income was reduced in later life from $16,000 to $8,000 and a person whose income in later life is only $3,000 but was reduced from a $4,000 previous level. Based on our findings, we would anticipate that the probability of having high morale is greater for the latter person, though he would be classified as poorer. (It is important to remember, however, that for the group of people who judge their incomes to be inadequate, there is a slight positive correlation between income size and morale.)

Life satisfaction, it would seem, suffers most from disjunctures in one's way of life. For those who have lived most of their lives at or near the poverty level, the relative decline in income after retirement is slight compared to those who witnessed a large income precipitously drop to something approximating officially designated poverty levels. For those in the latter situation, a large redefinition of needs must be part of their adjustment process if a reduced income is to be adequate for meeting those needs.

We also would suggest that, beyond any possible cohort effect, elderly people will tend to view money differently from the way they viewed it in their younger years. For most of society, including those people in our study, over much of their lives money is a measure of success and status as well as an instrument for acquiring physical security. For the elderly, generally, money is not likely to mean new opportunities or expanding horizons to the extent that it is for younger people. Among the continuing functions of money, certainly one of the most important to older people is that it is the primary means of holding on to familiar behavior patterns. The most crucial pattern for an older person in American society is to remain self-sufficient and to avoid becoming a burden to others, particularly one's children. In a sense, the older person thus avoids the onus of not having provided for an imminently foreseeable future.

Money is useful to people of all ages, of course. But the objective that its use is intended to achieve may be different for older people than for younger adults. For example, it permits a continuing tie to children and grandchildren through occasional gift-giving or other amenities. For a few, it might even permit older people to assume a supportive role at times when their children experience financial crisis or need. It may also be an important source of satisfaction in that it constitutes the "ultimate" legacy to one's children.

Because the relationships between INCOME , INCOME ADEQUACY and MORALE are quite complex we must further think of the determinants of INCOME ADEQUACY and some of the psychological determinants of MORALE which cannot be directly tested in this analysis. As noted previously, INCOME ADEQUACY encompasses much more than a simple accounting statement of income and expenditure balance. It also indirectly reflects an individual's ability to manage money. Those skilled in money management are more likely to have a surplus regardless of absolute income level than are those who handle money poorly. Thus, people with low incomes but good money management skills might well report high INCOME ADEQUACY while others with higher incomes but poorer budgetary skills report very low levels of INCOME ADEQUACY.

It is also important to remember that expenditures reflect a person's needs and desires and that these vary dramatically from one individual to another. For some, a trip to attend a grandson's Bar Mitzvah or wedding is a true need and dissatisfaction resulting from not being able to afford such a trip will negatively impact on MORALE, perhaps for a very long period of time. For others, such a trip might be only a weak desire and the inability to attend the occasion would not result in a strong feeling that one's income is inadequate. One can also imagine a similar situation arising with automobile maintenance, or the need to replace an old automobile, especially for those with fixed incomes during times of high inflation. Thus, what constitutes perceived needs is just as variable among individuals as is the amount of money available to meet those needs.

The path analysis results (Fig. 5.3) also indicate that RACE is positively related to INCOME ADEQUACY, revealing that whites report higher levels than do blacks. A similar situation was observed in considering CONDITION OF NEIGHBORHOOD. Although blacks report significantly lower mean annual incomes than do whites (Table 5.5) the difference is not consistent enough to result in a direct link between RACE and INCOME in the path model. Rather, we find that blacks as a group report lower levels of INCOME ADEQUACY. In part this may be due to differences in money management skills for this group, perhaps as a consequence of a narrow social and educational experience endemic to ghetto life. Another and perhaps more important factor may be the difficulties of optimizing income within an environment characterized by ghetto pricing and the remoteness of shopping alternatives. The latter explanation is certainly more in keeping with the earlier interpretation of the relationship between RACE and CONDITION OF NEIGHBORHOOD (see p. 119–20).

As has been seen, RACE also enters into other networks of relationships. Besides reporting lower income adequacy and poorer neighborhood environments than whites, blacks are more dependent on friends and neighbors. This may be due to the fact that older blacks have fewer children living in the local community or it may result from close social bonding among blacks in response to racial discrimination. It has also been shown that blacks have lower RELIGIOSITY scores than whites. Since high scores on our measure of religiosity were found primarily among whites living in relatively isolated social environments, we can again infer that strong levels of social interaction constitute a portion of the explanation for this finding.

As a group, then, we find that some of the same characteristics which constitute a special status for blacks of all ages also apply to older blacks. That is, the two principal manifestations of racial discrimination—economic discrimination and residential segregation—continue to affect blacks even in the latest stage of life. One might conclude from this that being black and being old create a double hardship in the lives of many older people. However, we find little direct evidence to support this. Rather, what is suggested is that many of the characteristics attending racial differences at younger ages are less apparent during old age. For example, whites who formerly provided their own transportation now must rely on others and public transit services. Many whites must adjust to post-retirement incomes near the poverty level. The fact that there is no significant difference in MORALE between whites and blacks, coupled with the fact that RACE enters into our analysis in only a very few places, reinforces the suggestion that socioeconomic characteristics which distinguish between races wane in importance during the later stages of life. The validity of this suggestion can only be ascertained in further research on minority groups within the elderly cohort.

In summary, then, our findings reveal two major independent dimensions of physical security: condition of one's neighborhood environment and financial security. The fact that the physical environment or neighborhood dimension is found to be related to MORALE independently from financial circumstances is significant for several reasons. First, it reinforces the findings of the preceding section of this chapter that neighborhood attributes directly affect the level of MORALE of older people. This is an area which has not been subjected to a great deal of rigorous analysis and consequently deserves considerable attention in future research. Second, it is apparent that many different elements within the neighborhood environment are significantly related to MORALE. Elements such as safety, appearance, stability, and the opportunity for social interaction vary from neighborhood to neighborhood. Such variations and relationships must be identified and analyzed if we are to understand fully the determinants of life satisfaction. Finally, the fact that neighborhood characteristics directly influence MORALE demonstrates that public policy makers, especially urban planners, who affect the nature of urban environments, can positively or negatively influence the level of life satisfaction of elderly persons in their communities. Obviously their influence extends well beyond the rather narrow limits of special programmatic efforts, such as nutrition and tax relief programs, designed to directly improve the lives of older people.

Our findings with respect to the second dimension of physical security, financial circumstances, also have significant policy implications. As we have seen, INCOME, as an absolute quantitative measure, has complex relationships with MORALE. For many people, larger incomes, if measured against a fixed level of needs, will positively influence INCOME ADEQUACY and consequently will lead to higher morale. For many others, particularly those with high incomes, INCOME is inversely related to MORALE. In such cases, income improvements will not influence MORALE. Moreover, there are many people scattered throughout the entire income spectrum for whom money is unimportant in determining or influencing life satisfaction. These results call into question the common perception that a policy of simply improving individual income will uniformly improve the quality of life for older people. (This conclusion is supported by Harris' findings that we discussed on pages 9–10).

The Mobility and Activity Network Within the General Urban Environment

The third network of environmental influences upon life satisfaction which emerges from this study also is composed of two dimensions, mobility and activities. Along both of these dimensions, the individual interacts with the general urban environment. Figure 5.4 reveals that both SELF-TRANSPORTATION and ACTIVITY impact directly on MORALE and that each is influenced by an individual's CAPACITY. Further, each is an intervening variable in a network of relationships leading to MORALE. As we pointed out in our discussion of the Capacity Network, ACTIVITY's direct impact on MORALE constitutes a different influence than is exerted by the SELF-TRANSPORTATION variable. The lack of a relationship between these two determinants of MORALE indicates that each dimension of this environmental network exerts a virtually independent influence on MORALE. Studies such as Cutler's and others conclude that transportation's impact upon levels of particular types of activity, e.g., "voluntary association participation," becomes significant among those elderly people who reside a long distance (greater than one half mile) away from such activity opportunities. However, such studies seldom control for intervening variables.[18] The measure of activity that emerged from our Guttman Scale analysis included, along with social participation indicators, hobbies, letter writing and visits by friends. While we believe that this broader measure of activity is more valuable in a study of life satisfaction, its breadth may serve to somewhat weaken a relationship between SELF-TRANSPORTATION and ACTIVITY. However, there are at least two other explanations for the discreteness of these two determinants. First of all, most of our

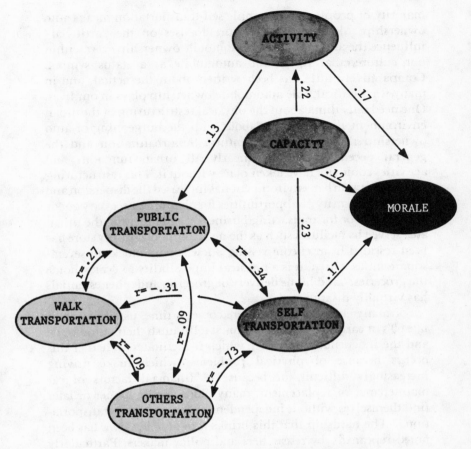

Figure 5.4 Mobility and Activity Network

sample reside in environments fairly rich in activity opportunities, which means that the ability to drive oneself is not as critical to social interaction as it may be in other environments. Also, in America auto driving is the primary symbol and means of remaining self-reliant.

In this chapter, we focus attention primarily on the SELF-TRANSPORTATION network, since CAPACITY and ACTIVITY have been dealt with extensively in Chapter 4. Much has been written about the importance of the automobile in our culture, and for the great majority of people in our sample self-transportation means auto ownership. Most of the literature focuses on the "artificial" influence the automobile and automobile ownership exert within our culture, that is, on the automobile as a status symbol. Comparatively little has been written about the actual, and in many ways critical, role automobile ownership plays in our lives. One need only think about the physical restructuring of the urban environment that has come about with the burgeoning of auto ownership throughout this century. Suburbanization and the general decentralization of nearly all urban functions and activities could not have taken place without it. This restructuring of the general urban environment has increased the dispersion and reduced the density of opportunities for obtaining necessary goods and services or for transacting business. Consequently, the urban area served by facilities such as the neighborhood grocery store has been rescaled from encompassing a few square blocks to several square miles. Often, it is a physical impossibility to "carry home the groceries," and home delivery of groceries and other essentials has virtually disappeared.

For many elderly persons, there comes a time, usually in their late 60's or early 70's, when they must relinquish their automobile and the independent mobility which it facilitates. Whether this occurs because of physical problems, which make driving increasingly difficult, or because of financial factors of car maintenance or replacement, many older people sooner or later find themselves without independent or self-provided transportation.[19] The hardship that this brings into people's lives has been noted repeatedly by researchers and policy makers. Particularly affected are those people who reside in small cities or in rural areas. Such hardship is also obviously brought into the lives of older persons who reside in neighborhoods of larger cities which are poorly or not at all served by mass public transit.[20] Surveys of elderly persons seeking their assessment of critical needs invariably list transportation as one of the top two or three problem areas.[21]

This situation was nicely summarized in the opening remarks at the 1970 White House Conference on Aging:

Without adequate transportation, a tremendous obstacle is imposed on the elderly, making it difficult for them to confront the simple tasks of living which they had previously taken for granted. Because of the serious lack of adequate intracity transportation, the elderly frequently abandon the idea of visiting relatives, senior citizen centers, and other social activities. Most shopping centers (excluding the Central Business District) are some distance from the center of town, and elderly citizens are unable to take advantage of bargains in supermarkets and discount stores, because there are no transportation facilities serving these centers.[22]

Our study demonstrates the significance of transportation mobility in the lives of older people via the direct link between SELF-TRANSPORTATION and MORALE shown in Figure 5.4. This network of relationships focuses upon SELF-TRANSPORTATION which measures one's ability to move independently about the general urban environment. The variable includes responses which indicate driving oneself to church, doctor's office, drug store, etc. Our other transportation variables relate to alternative transportation modes used in traveling to the same destinations.

Forty-eight percent of our sample indicate that they have high levels of SELF-TRANSPORTATION, and all but one percent of these are auto owners. This proportion is similar to that found in other large cities. The pattern of auto ownership among our sample is similar to that found in numerous other studies of elderly persons.[23] We find auto owners tend to be predominantly younger elderly, male, and married; and, as expected, they have greater financial resources. The relationships between SELF-TRANSPORTATION and the other transportation variables tend to be mutually exclusive. Those who report SELF-TRANSPORTATION seldom walk, use PUBLIC TRANSPORTATION, or rely on others. However, those who rely on others also walk and use public transportation.

There are important distinctions among those who do not report SELF-TRANSPORTATION, which is 52 percent of the sample. Of the entire sample, only 12.5 percent use PUBLIC TRANSPORTATION. As was noted earlier in this chapter, public transit serves only a very limited portion of the study area. Perhaps just as important is the fact that studies of elderly bus riders consistently indicate that bus systems, as they are most generally found in urban areas, are poor surrogates for auto ownership. Elderly riders often comment negatively on the frequency of service, location of routes, the inability to get where they wish to go and physical problems of walking, waiting, and transferring.[24] A substantial majority of non-auto owners in our sample rely on others for their transportation needs. Only seven percent of these also report public transportation usage as well as reliance on others. Walking is seldom engaged in by any group, although ten percent of those who rely on others and some of the public transportation users reported a few walking trips. In general, then, we find three virtually distinct groups: those who have self-transportation (48 percent); those who rely primarily on public transportation (12 percent—a few of these also rely on others); and a large group who depend entirely on others (40 percent). Thus, only half of our sample possesses the most desirable form of mobility within the urban environment.

The significance of SELF-TRANSPORTATION as an influence on MORALE is attributable to two interrelated explanations: mobility enhancement and independence maintenance. In the case of mobility enhancement, it is clear that one who owns an automobile, and has the physical capacity to use it, has available to him all of the activity opportunities offered in the general urban environment. It has been demonstrated repeatedly that auto owners report higher levels of trip terminations for all purposes outside the home.[25] Thus, self-transportation expands the physical limits of one's life space and facilitates attainment of many different types of activity opportunities.

A person who owns an automobile can determine where and when to engage in a wide variety of activities and need not rely on others. Moreover, he escapes the disturbing feeling of being a burden on others through his dependency. As Carp reports, loss of an automobile means the loss of independence, autonomy and self-sufficiency. These losses in turn increase indebtedness to others which becomes burdensome and demeaning when reciprocation is impossible.[26]

The dynamics of the relationship between SELF-TRANSPORTATION and MORALE require elaboration, however, since one cannot simply conclude, as does so much of the literature, that all older people without automobiles are relegated to a demeaning existence of limited mobility and indebtedness to others. Residential location within an urban environment structured for pedestrians rather than for automobiles has the salutary effect of reducing the need for automobile transportation. If necessary and desired activities within the environment are located close enough to one's residence, this obviously removes the need for vehicular transportation. Although it is unreasonable to expect a massive restructuring of the general urban environment to meet the needs of autoless elderly people, the proper siting of limited care and public housing projects for aging persons can enhance their immediate environments.[27]

Residential location with respect to the distribution of activity opportunities is important in other ways as well. As we have seen, older persons residing in neighborhoods with heavy concentrations of older people enjoy an enriched social environment. Visits to neighbors are probably more frequent and the likelihood that friends reside nearby is also enhanced. Since the importance of social trips for elderly people is second only to shopping trips (as measured by trip frequencies), providing oneself with such trips without requiring automobile ownership or reliance on others could be highly influential in maintaining self-reliance and related high morale. It should also be remembered that older people living in such neighborhood environments, at least in some parts of the city, likely have available to them public transportation, which, despite its obvious limitations and reported problems, does provide an alternative to total reliance on others.

Furthermore, it is possible that for many the loss of an auto and the concomitant reliance on others, which results in feelings of indebtedness, produces only a temporary decline in morale. Although one can no longer reciprocate in kind, i.e., provide transportation service, certainly other forms of reciprocity exist. Just as we have seen with other determinants of MORALE, the ability to adjust to changing circumstances engendered by declining self-sufficiency may be critical to maintaining an adequate level of life satisfaction.

Another factor which is often overlooked in studies of elderly people and their transportation needs is the fact that automobile ownership can place considerable stress upon a person's limited financial resources. In times of high inflation it is increasingly difficult to meet the costs of maintenance, insurance, and vehicle replacement. Moreover, driving itself becomes more complex with the advent of limited access expressways and greater levels of traffic congestion.

Despite these problems, however, for most people the sole means of acquiring self-transportation is automobile ownership. Auto ownership is important not only in maintaining the largest possible extent of one's life space, but it probably also has symbolic importance for older people just as it does for the larger population. It seems likely, however, that the symbolic importance of the automobile for older people is no longer that of success, achievement and status, but that of self-reliance.

The foregoing discussion indicates that the relation between self-transportation and life satisfaction is much more complex than is apparent from prior research which focuses primarily upon auto ownership. It is clear that life support and morale maintenance require high levels of mobility within the general urban environment as it is presently structured. It is also clear that the provision of such mobility, whether it be through auto ownership or some other means, should enhance rather than erode feelings of self-reliance.

In the light of our findings, we discuss in the following chapter programs and policies designed to ameliorate problems confronting older Americans. The delivery of transportation services is just one example of these programs. It is also apparent from the study results presented in this chapter, that policies and planning decisions which are not specifically targeted towards elderly persons, but which affect certain aspects of both the neighborhood and general urban environments, impact upon the quality of life of older urban residents.

Notes

1. Gregory Bateson, *Steps to an Ecology of Mind* (New York: Ballantine Books, 1972), pp. 315–20.

2. Louis Harris and Associates, Inc., *The Myth and Reality of Aging in America* (Washington, D.C.: National Council on Aging, Inc., 1975), p. 177.

3. Frances M. Carp, "Correlates of Mobility Among Retired Persons," *EDRA Two: Proceedings of the Second Annual Environmental Design Research Association Conference* (October 1970), pp. 171–82. F. Houston Wynn and Herbert S. Levinson, "Some Considerations in Appraising Bus Transit Potentials," *Highway Research Record*, No. 197: *Passenger Transportation*, Highway Research Board, NRC, 1967, 1–24.

4. Duane Marble, Perry O. Hanson, and Susan H. Hanson, "Intraurban Mobility Patterns of Elderly Households: A Swedish Example," *Proceedings of the Trans-*

portation Research Forum, First Conference on Transportation, Bruges, Belgium (1973), pp. 655-66.

5. *Ibid.,* p. 664.

6. For a review of such studies, as well as the author's own account, see Jaber F. Gubrium, *The Myth of the Golden Years,* (Springfield, Ill.: Charles C. Thomas, 1973), pp. 60-92.

7. Herbert J. Gans, "Planning and Social Life: Friendship and Neighbor Relations in Suburban Communities," *Journal of the American Institute of Planners,* vol. 27 (May 1961), pp. 134-40; Paul F. Lazarsfeld and Robert K. Merton, "Friendship as Social Process: A Substantive and Methodological Analysis," in Morroe Berger, Theodore Abel and Charles H. Page (eds.), *Freedom and Control in Modern Society* (New York: D. Van Nostrand Co., 1954), pp. 18-66; Gordon L. Bultena and Vivian Wood, "The American Retirement Community: Bane or Blessing?," paper presented at the annual meeting of the American Sociological Association, Denver, Colo., 1968; Mark Messer, "The Possibility of American Age-Concentrated Environment Becoming a Normative System," *The Gerontologist,* vol. 7 (1967), pp. 247-50; Irving Rosow, *Social Integration of the Aged* (New York: Free Press, 1967).

8. Irving Rosow, *Social Integration of the Aged* (New York: Free Press, 1967).

9. Gubrium, *op. cit.,* pp. 130-33.

10. For a consideration of widowhood and social deprivation, we refer the reader to the Lopata quotation on p. 66.

11. Bernard Kutner, David Fanshel, Alice Togo, and Thomas S. Langner, *Five Hundred Over Sixty: A Community Survey on Aging* (New York: Russell Sage Foundation, 1956).

12. Elmer Spreitzer and Eldon E. Snyder, "Correlates of Life Satisfaction Among the Aged," *Journal of Gerontology,* 29 (1974), pp. 454-58.

13. John N. Edwards and David L. Klemmack, "Correlates of Life Satisfaction: A Re-examination," *Journal of Gerontology,* vol. 28, no. 4 (1974), pp. 497-502.

14. Margaret Clark and Barbara G. Anderson, *Culture and Aging* (Springfield, Ill.: Charles C. Thomas, 1967), p. 219.

15. National figures are from the U.S. Bureau of the Census, 1970.

16. E. J. Cantilli and J. L. Schmelzer (eds.), *Transportation and Aging* (Washington, D.C.: U.S. Government Printing Office, 1971), pp. 100-107.

17. Spreitzer and Snyder, *op. cit.,* p. 455.

18. Stephen J. Cutler, "The Effects of Transportation and Distance on Voluntary Association Participation among the Aged," *International Journal on Aging and Human Development,* vol. 5, no. 1 (1974), pp. 81-94.

19. William L. Garrison, "Limitations and Constraints of Existing Transportation Systems as Applied to the Elderly," in E. G. Cantilli and J. L. Schmelzer (eds.), *Transportation and Aging* (U.S. Government Printing Office: Washington, D.C., 1971), p.102.

20. Frances M. Carp, "The Mobility of Retired People," in Cantilli and Schmelzer, pp. 26–27.

21. For an example of the high priority given to transportation problems even in a large city with relatively good public transit, see Bernice R. Bild and Robert J. Havighurst, "Senior Citizens in Great Cities: The Case of Chicago," *The Gerontologist*, vol. 11, Part II (February 1976), pp. 47–48.

22. Louis J. Pignataro, "Introduction," in Cantilla and Schmelzer (eds.), *op. cit.*, p. 4.

23. Joni Markovitz, "The Transportation Needs of the Elderly," in Cantilli and Schmelzer, *ibid.*, p. 68.

24. For a discussion of these factors see Garrison, *op. cit.*, pp. 100–106.

25. Carp, "Correlates of Mobility . . .," *op. cit.*; Markovitz, *op. cit.*; Cutler, *op. cit.*

26. Frances M. Carp, "Retired People as Automobile Passengers," *Gerontologist*, vol. 12 (Spring 1972), pp. 66–72.

27. Philadelphia City Planning Commission, *Locational Criteria for Housing for the Urban Elderly*, Internal Report (December 1968), pp. 4–8.

SIX

The Urban Elderly: Problems or Problem-Solvers?

Introduction

We began this study by listening to what older people had to say about their life experiences. We then structured these experiences on the basis of findings from previous social gerontological studies and examined relationships among them in order to understand better the dynamics of life satisfaction. This exploration into the life satisfaction of elderly urban residents, in turn, led us to a consideration of various aspects of the aging process. While our findings tend to support some of the commonly-held beliefs about aging, they also indicate that many others require modification or even replacement. More importantly, we have seen in the preceeding chapters that the condition of elderly people in a modern society involves complex social and psychological systems in which a myriad of factors interact with one another.

In Chapters 4 and 5, we examine closely the interaction among constituents of life satisfaction, both personal and environmental. We also offer explanations for the manner in which these constituents combine into networks of relationships that bear upon the quality of life of the urban elderly. In the present chapter, we explore the implications of the entire range of our findings as they relate to the state of social gerontological theory today. Furthermore, we examine the relation between life satisfaction and the problem-solving ability of elderly people. From this examination we propose a new social and psychological perspective on the aging process, which we believe can contribute to the search for a comprehensive policy toward older Americans.

Life Satisfaction and Social Gerontological Theories of Aging

A reappraisal of social gerontological theory in light of our research leads us now to view the field as having generated at least two paradigms encompassing four perspectives on the aging process. One paradigm emphasizes the *special status* of the elderly and, correspondingly, discontinuity with characteristics of middle-age life. The other emphasizes the predisposition of aging persons to maintain behaviors of earlier adulthood, thus stressing continuity with the past.

The special status paradigm includes "disengagement theory" and what may be termed "subcultural theory." As the term implies, the subcultural perspective portrays aging people as evolving into a distinct subgroup within society. Two conditions underlie this perspective, one physical and one social. The physical capacity of the individual inevitably declines with advancing age. In addition, all people of advanced age have experienced some loss of social roles. Societal response to these imperatives of old age is such that it engenders a consensus about the nature of the older person that may be expressed in subtle (e.g., anticipated mental decline) or notso-subtle (e.g., mandatory retirement) ways. Since individual physical decline, the loss of social roles, and social stereotypes distinguish the older person from other adults, discontinuity with previous life is forced upon those of advanced age.

While disengagement theory ascribes special status to the elderly, it also includes the participation of the aging individual in the process of mutual withdrawal. That is, the old person withdraws from society as well as society from the old person, in preparation for the person's inevitable and impending death. Although individuals may experience disengagement at different times and under varying circumstances, the process as a whole is thought to lead ultimately to the same condition, which thereby constitutes a special status for the elderly.

The continuity paradigm of aging is represented by "activity theory" and by "continuity theory." According to "activity theory," older people will persist as long as possible in sustaining the familiar patterns of their middle age. This perspective would seem to apply only to those elderly people who, by virtue of continued good health and financial security, can maintain their previous ways of living. Since we know that both income and physical condition tend to decline with advancing age, it is likely that only a small portion of those of advanced age can meet both of these criteria and thus fall within the purview of activity theory.

On the other hand, according to "continuity theory," it is possible for the individual to maintain habitual patterns of behavior and value orientations by adapting these to the contingencies of old age. That is, the underlying nature of one's experience may be sustained, although the form of that experience may have to be modified. Therefore, this concept could include virtually all old people. Of course, the possible adjustments that the older person might make to his changing world are quite extensive. The appeal of this relatively positive approach to aging is that it attributes to the individual a never-ending capacity for adaptive change. The optimistic character of this approach perhaps accounts for the fact that it is increasingly embraced by social gerontologists.

At the same time that "continuity theory" has enjoyed increasing popularity, special status perspectives have been relegated more and more to the position of myths and misconceptions about aging. To this extent we see a potential paradigmatic shift occurring in social gerontology today. While we believe that this shift is not unwarranted, we have reason to suspect that it would be unrealistic to ignore the import of special status characteristics.

Included in our findings is supporting evidence for elements of both paradigms of the aging process. As one example of special status characteristics found in our study, physical condition, represented by CAPACITY, predictably declines as age advances and the decline is precipitous for the older elderly. To illustrate: 5 percent of our sample between the ages of 70 and 74 reported that they needed help in sweeping or vacuuming. At the same time, 54 percent of our sample 85-89 needed help. Considering a more rigorous task, 54 percent of those 70-74 needed help mowing the lawn, while 93 percent of those 85–89 needed assistance with this task. All of which demonstrates that the general decline in physical capacity experienced by people in their later years imposes a special condition upon the elderly when it comes to performing fundamental life-support activities.

Some support also was found for the disengagement perspective (special status) in that the desire for social contact with other people tends to weaken with advancing age. This is seen in the inverse relationship between AGE and SOCIAL ATTITUDE in our analysis. That portion of disengagement theory postulating the individual's participation in the withdrawal process is therefore given some support.

A further example of special status involves dependence on one's family. Americans are socialized to resist becoming dependent, but the positive relationship between AGE and DEPENDENCE ON FAMILY suggests that older people find it especially difficult to live by this social value. While modern social life requires a high degree of interdependency among all people, the dependent relationship that develops in extreme old age often borders on helplessness; therefore, it conforms more closely to the pejorative social definition of dependency. That is, the older person's dependence on his family is more elemental, and reciprocation of assistance is more difficult.

At the same time that our findings reinforce the presence of some special status characteristics, we also find evidence supporting the continuity paradigm. The precepts of continuity theory, for example, help to explain our findings about the activities of older people. While the specific activities considered most meaningful by older people often change during later life, there is a strong tendency for the new activities to embody the underlying orientations of the activities of middle age. For men, the underlying orientation tends to be productivity and problem-solving, exemplified in later life by hobby activities. For women it is the maintenance of social institutions, in early life the family and in later life the church. There is also for women the continuation of nurturant social behavior found in child rearing in earlier life and in interaction with neighbors in later years.

We have already mentioned that the kind of dependency to

which older people are subject creates for them a special status. At the same time, the older individual's continued struggle to maintain the ideal of self-reliance is another indication of the continuity perspective. One of the strongest instruments and symbols of self-reliance in America is the automobile. Older people, like Americans of all ages, value the ability to maintain self-transportation. Self-rated health also falls within the continuity context, since it does not decline with age as one would expect it to; rather, the processes of self-rating remain more or less constant throughout life. First, people at any age tend to rate their health relative to the perceived health of their peers. Second, self-rated health and morale are interdependent: if a person of any age perceives his life in generally optimistic terms, then he is likely to evaluate his health more favorably than his objective condition might warrant. This is confirmed by even the oldest people in our sample.

As the foregoing discussion demonstrates, we are able to explain certain of our findings by applying the special status perspectives, and certain other findings by employing continuity perspectives. However, some of our findings can only be explained if we employ both types simultaneously.

We have found, as have other scholars, that old people, much as any age group, derive satisfaction from living near those whom they consider to be most like themselves. While this suggests continuity, special status is also indicated, in that age itself increases in importance as a criterion of "likeness," until it may perhaps become the dominant criterion.[1] Earlier residential preference is often determined by socioeconomic status, professional identification, or quality of schools, all of which have diminished markedly in importance for the older person.

It has been well-documented that as a group, older people have substantially smaller incomes than do younger age cohorts. Further, in our sample of older people, income size declines with age. Special status is also indicated in that the meaning of money probably changes with advancing age. To some extent, money always represents security. For the younger person, however, the major significance of money generally lies in its potential for expanding opportunities, upward social mobility, and material acquisition. For the older individual, the meaning of money increasingly lies in its ability to insure physical and emotional security, and in some cases, survival. Our interpretation of the relation between income and life satisfaction indicates that given income "adequacy," those older people who have suffered the greatest decline in income relative to their middle years have the lowest levels of life satisfaction. In this interpretation, it is consistency with one's previous financial status, rather than income size, that contributes to life satisfaction in old age.

Sex differences also illustrate the interplay between continuity and special status paradigms. Women in our sample are more dependent on their families than are men. We assume that for this cohort, women were always more dependent on kinship ties. Similarly, women of all ages tend to be more vulnerable than men to physical attack and, therefore, are more apprehensive about their immediate environments, particularly at night. However, we find that as the capacity of men to protect themselves declines with advancing age, they become as fearful as women about their surroundings. To this extent, then, age imposes a special status mitigating sexual differences.

In summary, we have shown that some of our findings can be explained by using exclusively either a special status or a continuity view of aging, while still others are best explained by using both paradigms at once. This reflects the complex realities of old age that are not adequately explained by any single theory of aging. Each perspective does express, however, a valid dimension of the aging process. It is our contention that an adequate theory of life satisfaction in old age will have to integrate the special status and continuity models. The fact that a number of critical variables influencing life satisfaction straddle both indicates that they are to some extent correlated, and that the development of an integrative model is possible.

A clue to the direction one might take in developing an integrative model emerged from a profile analysis of our sample. Along with the regression analyses, we conducted a discriminant analysis on a portion of the sample, to discover that combination of traits that best distinguished those with high morale from those with low morale (high morale being defined as the top one-third of the morale scores, and low morale as the bottom one-third). In this analysis, the combination of traits (called the discriminant function) distinguished strongly between respondents with high morale and those with low morale. If, for instance, we were to predict high or low morale scores on the basis of the values derived from the function alone, this prediction would have been correct 86 percent of the time. Table 6.1 shows the results of this analysis.[2]

Table 6.1   Discriminate Function*

+ Direction		– Direction	
Cope	.34	Income Size	.20
Capacity	.32	Relatives in K.C.	.19
Medical	.26	Residential Mobility	.18
Education	.22	Transportation from Others	.15
Living with Someone	.16		
Media Use	.15		

*Canonical correlation = .72
Wilks' Lambda = .48   p < .001

Generally the strongest variable is used to name the function because it best identifies the underlying meaning. Other variables that are part of the function can be interpreted on the basis of that meaning. The single trait that contributes most to this discriminant function is the ability to cope with problems (COPE). It should be recalled that COPE measures the extent to which the individual possesses specialized information appropriate to solving legal, medical and consumer problems. People having the ability to cope with this type of problem will also be able to deal effectively with a wide variety of problems requiring less specialized information. The positive column in Figure 6.1 consists of coping resources. There are two principal types of resources: EDUCATION and MEDIA USE represent sources of knowledge, while CAPACITY and MEDICAL represent the physical mobility necessary to implement action directed by that knowledge. LIVING WITH SOMEONE is also part of this column since it can enhance one's physical mobility as well as increase one's reservoir of knowledge. It also extends other individual resources and permits the sharing of everyday burdens with another person.

The remaining variables (in the right-hand column) are inversely related to the above coping resources. The strongest negative contribution to the function is INCOME, which corresponds to the negative influence INCOME exerts on MORALE in the path analysis. The unexpected role that income again plays, with respect to our sample, suggests that its effect on the lives of older people is more complex than is generally assumed. A thorough clarification of these complexities requires further research designed to exercise controls over a broad range of intervening variables and perhaps cohort differences. At the same time, the results of our analyses shed some light on these complexities and indicate the directions such research might take.

The present findings should not be interpreted as indicating that the poor are better off than the more affluent. Sociological literature thoroughly documents the problems associated with poverty status. Our findings, rather, direct attention to the impact that income reduction in later life has on one's ability to cope with problems.

As was the case in the analysis of income's negative impact on life satisfaction, we suggest that economic class differentials have a bearing on income's relation to the coping function. The relatively wealthy person, of any age, will be accustomed to purchasing the skills of others who, professionally or otherwise, do that person's coping. Such a person will also be able to retain a high enough income after retirement to continue commanding such services. Low-income people, on the other hand, having had far less ability to purchase services, will have lived with the necessity of developing their own coping strategies. This may represent longterm training for survival with comparatively meager financial resources. With respect to problem-solving skills, then, middle-income people may be affected most by income reduction following retirement. While their ability to solve problems by using financial resources is significantly reduced, they are, at the same time, less likely than poorer people to have acquired surrogate coping skills.

Of course, in individual cases, such factors as education, expectations and motivation will intervene in this process. It is also possible that sex and marital status will prove to be significant intervening variables. For example, the older middle-class widow, previously assisted by husband and purchasing power, may find herself unequipped to cope with the problems usually associated with poverty status.

RELATIVES IN KC is the next strongest negative contribution to the coping function. The close geographic proximity of relatives represents a potential source of information and physical assistance in solving problems. Therefore, people lacking this source find it more difficult to cope with their problems. Using the coping skills of others poses a difficulty for the older person, the erosion of self-reliance. If a person cannot remain self-reliant, his life satisfaction will suffer accordingly. This is also indicated by the inverse relationship between transportation from others and the ability to cope. The reliance on others for transportation not only reflects a state of dependency, but also may represent for some a decline in self-reliance from a time when they were able to provide their own transportation.

Finally, a high rate of residential change represents, for many, ineffectual attempts to cope with a variety of problems. As a group, older people are the most residentially stable; but some undergo frequent changes of address which cannot be accounted for strictly by forced moves. Chronic movers of all ages frequently give the same reasons for each of their repeated moves. Although it might appear that they are solving their problems by relocating, in fact they are attempting to escape from problems that only follow them to the next address.[3] Thus, the development of effective coping skills eludes them.

In looking at the traits that most sharply differentiate people with high morale from those with low morale, we have seen that the variable ABILITY TO COPE WITH PROBLEMS is related to a wide complex of other problem-solving resources. Although this problem-solving function is derived from a reduced sample, it clearly corresponds to the results of the path analyses. The ABILITY TO COPE WITH PROBLEMS, CAPACITY, MEDICAL and INCOME are direct determinants of MORALE in the path analysis and are important contributors to the problem-solving dimension that emerges from the discriminant analysis. While the other constituents of life satisfaction are not specifically represented in the discriminant function, their correlates are present. Self-reliance is represented by SELF-TRANSPORTATION in the path model and obversely by

TRANSPORTATION FROM OTHERS in the coping function. In the same sense, the rate of residential mobility reflects, to some extent, the condition of one's neighborhood. Furthermore, the resource represented by living in an age-concentrated neighborhood substitutes for the resource represented by living with someone in the same home. The size of one's income is negatively associated with the coping function in the same way that INCOME negatively relates to life satisfaction in the path analysis when INCOME ADEQUACY is held constant. Social participation (ACTIVITY) is important to life satisfaction, and its contribution to the problem-solving dimension is through COPE, CAPACITY, and EDUCATION, all of which impact on ACTIVITY in the path model. For this reason, it does not appear in the discriminant analysis. In sum, we can augment our understanding of the path analyses by viewing them from this more integrative coping perspective.

The Ability to Cope with Problems: A Perspective on Theory

The variable COPE, which measures knowledge useful for solving specific problems, is a direct determinant of life satisfaction not usually specifically identified as such in previous studies. In the preceding section our conceptualization of coping was expanded through a discriminant analysis, the results of which articulated a broader dimension of problem-solving behavior. This conception is consonant with the contemporary understanding of coping recognized by behavioral scientists. As Coelho, *et al.*, have stated:

> Research on coping behavior emphasized processes of human problem-solving in the direction of adaptive change. It brings into focus transactions of individuals or groups that are effective in meeting the requirements or utilizing the opportunities of specific environments. It highlights possibilities for enhancing the competence of individuals through developmental attainments, including ways of learning from exceptionally difficult circumstances. It is also beginning to suggest ways in which such stressful circumstances may be modified to diminish human suffering.[4]

Through the coping perspective we can view the theories of aging discussed earlier as diverse and frequently occurring responses to old age. In other words, each of these theories will be re-interpreted here as a particular type of coping strategy. The subcultural theory suggests that individuals cope with growing old primarily by acquiescing to the assumptions underlying the American folk philosophy about old age. As we interpret it, this response is essentially a passive one. At the same time, the events that create subcultural status for the aging individual are predominantly of a stressful nature, e.g., loss of job, loss of spouse, and loss of health.

In activity theory, the individual is guided by the same folk philosophy, but responds by avoiding the onset of stereotypical old age as long as possible through perpetuation of middle-aged behavior. The underlying premise here is that old age is an unattractive period of life; therefore, the person's attitude is essentially as acquiescent regarding the folk philosophy as it is with the subculture strategy. The activity strategy is by and large less stressful than the subcultural one for those who have retained the resources of middle age—an adequate income, health, satisfying social relations, *etc.*—than for those with fewer resources. Nevertheless, the strategy will eventually become stressful since middle-aged behavior cannot be sustained indefinitely.

Disengagement can be looked at as a way of growing old gracefully given the mandates of the folk philosophy that older people should step aside for younger generations. When an individual experiences one or more traumatic events characterizing special status in old age or when declining resources render it impossible to continue middle-age behaviors, disengagement becomes a viable coping strategy. Thus, it is a strategy conceived under stress which allows the old person to concentrate on the few roles that can still be successfully performed. However, this behavior is congruent with societal expectations and/or requirements. While this strategy would not be adopted by every individual, nor would it be employed by everyone at the same age, it is a reasonable strategy under certain circumstances for maintaining satisfaction in the later years.

Continuity theory is the least researched of the approaches to aging discussed here. Because its definition of aging results in a very general characterization of the process, it is possible to apply it in such a diffuse manner as to dilute its value as a tool for explanation. As the model is often presented, its basic tenet of continuity with previous behavior patterns and value orientations can be applied to individuals at any period in the life cycle. Also, the principal of adaptation, if taken to the extreme of including dramatic redefinitions of assumptions which alter the individual's perception of reality, negates the central notion of continuity with the past.

People share an underlying need to continue familiar patterns of thought and action,[5] and continuity theory suggests how this need can be met, through adaptive behavior. In employing the theory, however, emphasis should be placed on the adjustments people make in their activities. (It is after all, a variant of activity theory.) A major task of the researcher using continuity theory, then, is to demonstrate the link between the previous and the new behavior. Since the new behavior will depend on psychological adaptation to the conditions of advanced age, this demonstration will require further theoretical development of the psychological dimensions of coping behavior. Recent work in experimental psychology by Holmes, Houston and others, which examines how individuals cope with stress, may provide directions for such theoretical development.[6]

For purposes of explaining how older people cope with life's problems, the continuity perspectives seem most appropriate to situations involving relatively little stress. This is so because, among other reasons, it implies fairly long-term planning for the purpose of avoiding stress and because successful adaptation implies possession of sufficient resources to keep options open for the individual.[7] The special status perspectives appear to be more appropriate to situations of high stress engendered by a traumatic event or by the accumulation of traumatic events in later life. However, as we have pointed out, the psychological underpinnings of the special status concepts require considerable development.

Viewing the theories of aging in terms of coping behavior suggests that they may be integrated along dimensions of stress level and degree of individual initiative. We offer this typology only as a basis for hypothesis construction. While it flows logically from the analysis presented in this work, it is obvious that the relationships expressed here need to be tested by further research.

Such research would further delineate the various domains and clarify the respective contributions of these theories.

As the theories are arrayed in Figure 6.1, they continue to reflect the two major paradigms discussed earlier. In that discussion, we suggested that a paradigmatic shift is occurring in social gerontology from an emphasis on the socio-cultural influence in the aging process to an emphasis on individual adaptations to aging. This is consistent with the broader shift occurring in the social sciences from an aggregate research perspective to a focus on individual behavior. The theories constituting the continuity paradigm, then, assume high levels of initiative on the part of the

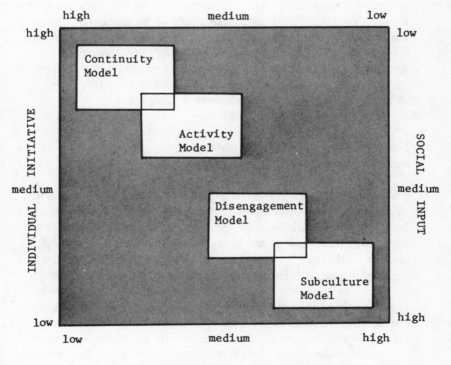

Figure 6.1 Typology of Aging Models as Coping Strategies with Resources Held Constant

adapting individual, while the special status theories involve a higher degree of social and cultural input. These latter theories are strategies for coping with the less frequent but most critical events of old age. The continuity strategies, on the other hand, allow the individual to cope with less severe, day-to-day problems. The coping perspective, therefore, relates the level of stress in the events of later life to the respective models of both paradigms.

Coping ability, at least as it relates to the life satisfaction of the urban elderly, not only adds a dimension to our understanding of the aging process, but it also enables us to integrate the various theories of aging that have been previously developed. Each of these theories can be understood as a particular strategy for coping with the problems of old age. Thus, rather than being seen as competing models of the social aspects of aging, they may be viewed as complementary. The coping perspective we are suggesting modifies in two ways the long-standing problem orientation of the field of social gerontology. First, it recognizes a range of problem types that may be arrayed on a "stress" continuum. Second, it suggests a more active role for the individual confronting the problems of old age.

The Ability to Cope with Problems: Policy Implications

The specific behaviors that older people develop for coping with problems will depend not only on their own internal capabilities but also on the availability of resources in their environment (e.g., shopping opportunities, medical clinics, relatives and friends, *etc.*) and on facilitating mechanisms provided by the society at large (e.g., information referral, transportation, counselling and other services). In the context of problem-solving, facilitating mechisms constitute the interface between individual capabilities and environmental resources. These mechanisms may be directed at aiding the individual to cope with either the more critical events of old age contributing to special status or the less severe day-to-day problems.

Most physical and social environmental resources in this society are developed by the private sector and are distributed without reference to the needs of old people. Therefore, the most feasible and effective contribution that government can make to the life satisfaction of the elderly is through the provision of facilitating mechanisms. Recently, the federal government has introduced a variety of programs designed to deliver specific services to elderly citizens and at the same time has maintained the older social welfare programs. These programs may be considered in terms of the major constituents of life satisfaction identified in this study.

Driving an automobile is one of the most fundamental mechanisms in this society for satisfying individual needs, providing mobility to acquire both the necessities and amenities of life. When self-transportation is no longer possible, older people must rely on other individuals or on organized transportation services. The federal government has responded to this need by funding senior citizen reduced-fare programs and "dial-a-ride" services. However, besides its mobility function, self-transportation meets the individual's need to live up to the cultural value of self-reliance, and a satisfactory transportation system should meet both of these needs simultaneously. Mass transit systems provide more independence of movement than is achieved by relying on others for rides, but have been criticized for not meeting the special mobility needs of older people. "Dial-a-ride" minibus systems, while meeting mobility needs, unfortunately convey the stigma of social welfare. Para-transit service, principally in the form of taxi subsidization, meets both needs but is the most costly program thus far undertaken.

The health needs of older people have been addressed by two types of government programs. The first type subsidizes health care through direct payments to providers (Medicare and Medicaid). The second type, a more recent development, delivers medical services of a more preventative nature through such programs as health screening and congregate meals. These programs may be contributing significantly to health maintenance in old age, but ultimately physical decline is unavoidable. A person who is unable to perform the fundamental tasks of daily life must either relinquish residential independence (by moving to a nursing home or to the home of a relative) or receive assistance with such household tasks. Such services to the home as "meals on wheels" and "homemaker" are partial solutions to the problem but are not alone sufficient to preserve residential independence.

The individual's need for social participation has been taken into account by, among other things, federal funding for senior centers. As we have seen, interaction with other people is a primary means of obtaining information that helps the older person cope with problems. Specific problem solving information is often made available directly to the older person through the information referral services of local area agencies on aging. However, these services seldom include counselling that enables the older person to independently develop coping strategies.

Social security and supplementary income payments represent, of course, the government's contribution to the income base of older citizens. Indeed, for many older people, it is the major source of income. While it is essential that our society ensure an adequate level of income for all older people, we have found that the actual size of an older person's income has a complex relation to life satisfaction. In formulating programs that provide financial assistance for the elderly, this complexity should not be overlooked.

We have also found a strong environmental component of life satisfaction, represented by the condition of one's neighborhood and the concentration of elderly people within it. The federal government can, and does, fund programs designed to improve deteriorating neighborhoods, the Community Development Block Grant provisions being an excellent example. However, in matters most directly affecting old people—such as the safety, appearance, and the age structure of the neighborhood, as well as accessibility to services—responsibility rests almost exclusively at the local level. That is, the disposition of such matters will depend upon the decisions of local officials, civic leaders, and private businessmen. By and large, local response to these needs of older people has been far from adequate.

Two generalizations can be made from this brief review of policy toward the aged. The first involves a basic shift in policy emphasis. Income and health maintenance programs were the first to be emphasized by the federal government. In general, such programs are intended to help older people deal with the consequences of special status events, e.g., retirement and chronic health problems. A more recent emphasis has been placed on preventative measures and on helping people cope with more commonplace problems. Another way of describing the changing emphasis is from life support objectives to life enrichment objectives. This policy shift parallels, although it probably lags behind, the paradigmatic shift in gerontological thought that we discussed earlier; in other words, it parallels the change in emphasis from special status to continuity theories of aging.

The second generalization concerns the consequences of government policy. Whether successful or not, government programs for the most part have aimed at maintaining the independence of the older citizen. This goal may not be explicitly stated for it grows out of American society's orientation toward self-reliance. Our findings, of course, have suggested that self-reliance or independence is an important element in the life satisfaction of the elderly. At the same time, it is clear that a satisfying life is also predicated on personal competence in dealing with day-to-day problems. A person is most likely to retain feelings of competence and efficacy if he or she acquires conceptual skills that facilitate the development of coping strategies. More emphasis, therefore, should be placed on helping the older individual acquire such skills, although this is a more difficult task than simply providing the resources necessary for remaining independent. We are suggesting, then, that government should not simply solve old people's problems, but further, it should help old people learn how to solve their own problems.

To some extent, conceptual skills may be learned through direct counselling (or other tutorial methods) for the aged, as for any other group. In addition to these programmatic mechanisms, more informal activities may also contribute to a person's problem-solving skills. As we have seen, social participation enhances one's ability to cope with problems. However, it is evident that for most people, conceptual skills for problem solving can only be acquired over a long period of time. Preparation for dealing with the kinds of problems that confront people in old age will require a conscious, societal effort carried out on many levels. As Lowenthal has pointed out in a somewhat different context:

> What is needed is a life-course orientation in all of our social, educational, and economic institutions, one which will have its impact

on adolescents and young adults, so that, when they approach the twenty- or thirty-year postparental stage, they will not be forced to project as empty a future as do most people who now make up the postparental and retirement cohorts.[8]

Conclusion

A major difficulty inherent in the aging process in our society is the conflict between persisting personal values and changing social expectations. It is particularly interesting that young Americans are, in a sense, encouraged to be dissatisfied with their lives at any given point. They are supposed to "improve" their lives: become better educated, move to better neighborhoods, acquire better jobs, purchase better products, achieve greater authority, and so on. But when Americans reach a relatively advanced age, they are expected to stop achieving. At this time in life, the socially prescribed ideal state is one of contentment. In other words, older Americans are left with a single goal, to adjust successfully to the contingencies of old age.

It is, perhaps, this attitude toward old age that underlies social actions toward the aged. As our discussion of policy indicates, such actions tend principally to underwrite the prescribed contentment of older people by attempting to solve their problems. This is in marked contrast to social policies toward the problems of youth. Programs such as Head Start and Upward Bound are designed to instill in the young person the conceptual skills and information necessary to avoid, or successfully handle, life's problems. The fundamental objective of such programs for young people is essentially preventative in that they equip the individual to solve problems without continuing societal support. Programs for the elderly, in contrast, presume continuous and even increasing societal support. This presumption casts the older individual in the role of passive and permanent recipient of social welfare benefits. An alternative assumption on which social policy toward the elderly might be based is that older people can actively participate in the problem-solving process.

Accepting the older person as an active, though not always successful, problem solver (rather than as a passive beneficiary) necessitates adjusting specific policies, changing social definitions of acceptable behavior among older people, and modifying somewhat social gerontological research. Future policy would have to place more emphasis on life-enrichment programs such as life-course planning in public and continuing education, pre-retirement planning, life adjustment counselling following loss, and avocation training. In addition to these programs, we must initiate training procedures that would help the individual develop strategies for successfully using the resources available in the immediate environment. Instituting these life enrichment programs in no way eliminates the need to continue present programs designed to solve major problems of old age. These problems derive less from personal ineptitude or failure in coping with life's difficulties than from the adverse effects of social forces (attitudinal and/or organizational) which frustrate an elderly individual's successful coping. We feel that it is through the development of coping skills, and hence feelings of efficacy and competence, that the life satisfaction of elderly people can be enhanced most dramatically. The steps we are proposing, then, will not reduce the government's financial commitment to the elderly, at least in the immediate future. It is possible in the long run, however, that this approach will prove less costly than current programs projected into the future, given predicted demographic trends.

Public perception of old people and the aging process is becoming more realistic, aided perhaps by the increased attention being paid to circumstances surrounding old age by academicians, government officials, and journalists. However, to maximize the individual's potential for a satisfying life in later years, the public (including older people themselves) must further develop realistic expectations regarding acceptable ways in which older people may structure their lives. For example, a rejection of the attitude that the economically unproductive person is a worthless person would benefit older people immensely. The lives of many older people today are plagued by the felt necessity of contributing substantively to society in lieu of earning a living. The idea that activities may simply be self-centered is not entirely acceptable, particularly among older people. In answer to our open-ended question regarding the most rewarding activities in later years, many people included among their responses "helping others," or "being useful to somebody" (note Mrs. Fremont's comments on page 2). The vagueness of these answers suggests a deference to the principle of productivity, rather than participation in a specific helping situation.

Another example of a beneficial attitudinal change would be the acceptance of more flexible living arrangements for older people. Our findings indicate that either being married or living with a relative or friend increases substantially one's coping ability, and therefore one's life satisfaction. But what are the prospects for the older person who, through separation or death, is faced with living alone? Marriage is a viable alternative for only a few, partly because of demographic realities and partly because of social inhibitions. For a substantial majority, the only feasible alternative is a single existence. Increasingly, however, single older people are choosing semi-congregate living arrangements such as apartment complexes designed for more affluent older people and public housing projects for those who are less affluent. This indicates a strong preference for age-concentrated living arrangements, which corresponds to our finding that % ELDERLY impacts on life satisfaction. This impulse toward communal living is not fully recognized by society and indeed is frustrated by currently acceptable living arrangements.

A more positive public attitude toward communal forms of living would allow greater flexibility for the older individual in choosing living arrangements appropriate to particular needs. There are also many instances in which older individuals could benefit from a form of cohabitation that did not require a life-long commitment. By pooling their resources, two people might be able to cope with the problems of old age better than they could alone. Yet, neither may be willing to assume total responsibility for the other person for life. Adjustments in social expectations regarding the elderly would, in sum, expand the range of options available to people for solving the problems that attend old age.

While studying people living in special housing for the elderly, Lawton and his associates articulated the "environmental docility hypothesis."[9] Essentially, the hypothesis states that the less competent the individual, the more that individual's behavior will be affected by his environment. By "competent" they meant the possession of personal resources such as socioeconomic status, physical health, social integration, ego strength, and intelligence. Their measure of behavior was friendship formation and the environment was confined to the building in which the individuals resided. Thus, people who were relatively less competent tended to form friendships on the basis of proximity to their living units rather than on other bases applicable to people of relatively high competence. Our findings indicate that this hypothesis may also apply to elderly people living in more typical urban residential settings. CAPACITY was positively related to CONDITION OF NEIGHBORHOOD in the path analysis. This demonstrates that, in general, people with low capacity regard their neighborhoods negatively and are particularly concerned with neighborhood safety.

While our findings tend to support the relation between environment and individual hypothesized by Lawton, we believe that an emphasis on "docility" can inadvertently bias our conception of old age. As we have seen, older people are capable of developing coping strategies that may overcome at least some adversity, and those that do are generally more satisfied with their lives. Future research, therefore, might increase our understanding of the relationship between the individual and the environment if it takes into account the older person's potential for active problem-solving. For example, the inverse relationship between individual competence and the impact of the environment on the individual may be mitigated by knowledge of, and use of, coping mechanisms provided by the society. Also, the influence of the environment may be reduced by the creative use of informal coping mechanisms such as cooperative living arrangements, neighboring, and voluntary association participation.

We have been examining in some detail the constituents of life satisfaction. The ability to cope with problems has emerged from this analysis as a particularly important dimension of life satisfaction among the urban elderly today. But what of the future? Social observers generally are in agreement that, given present trends, older people not only will constitute an increasingly greater proportion of the population, but also as a group will exhibit a different profile. Among other changes, the elderly of the future will be much better educated and to some extent healthier. A less physically restricted and more highly informed elderly population, on the average, will possess a greater potential for effectively coping with life's problems. Therefore, theories of aging, as well as policies toward the elderly, built on the assumption that older individuals can and do formulate effective problem-solving strategies will be even more cogent in the years ahead.

Notes

1. For a thorough discussion of friendship relations, see Beth Hess, "Friendship," in Riley, *et al.* (eds.), *Aging and Society: Vol. 3, A Sociology of Age Stratification* (New York: Russell Sage Foundation, 1972), pp. 357–93.

2. All variables used in the regression analysis are included in this analysis. Only the strongest variables are shown in the table, however. All other variables have relatively low coefficients compared to these.

3. Forrest J. Berghorn and Ronald C. Naugle, *Changing Residence in Kansas City, Kansas: The Geographic and Socioeconomic Bases of Urban Mobility* (Kansas City, Mo.: Mid-American Urban Observatory, 1973), pp. 60–62.

4. George V. Coelho, David Hamburg, and John E. Adams, "Synthesis of Biological and Social Perspectives," in Coelho, *et al.* (eds.), *Coping and Adaptation* (New York: Basic Books, Inc., 1974), p. 440.

5. For a detailed discussion of this need, see Gardner Murphy, *Personality: A Bio-Social Approach to Origins and Structure* (New York: Harper and Brothers, 1946), Chapter 8, for Murphy's analysis of the canalization process.

6. See, for example, David S. Holmes and B. Kent Houston, "Effectiveness of Situation Redefinition and Affective Isolation in Coping with Stress," *Journal of Personality and Social Psychology*, vol. 29 (1974), pp. 212–18; Larry Bloom, *et al.*, "The Effectiveness of Attentunal Diversion and Situation Redefinition for Reducing Stress Due to a Nonambiguous Threat," *Journal of Research in Personality*, vol. 11 (1977), pp. 83–94; David S. Holmes, "Compensation for Ego Threat: Two Experiments," *Journal of Personality and Social Psychology*, vol. 18 (1973), pp. 234–37; Reuven Gal and Richard Lazarus, "The Role of Activity in Anticipating and Confronting Stressful Situations," in Coelho, *et al., op. cit.*

7. Gordon F. Streib, "Retirement: Crisis or Continuities?" in Carter C. Osterbind (ed.), *Migration, Mobility and Aging* (Gainesville, Fla.: Center for Gerontological Studies and Programs, University of Florida, 1975), p. 23.

8. Marjorie Fiske Lowenthal, Majda Thurnher, David Chiriboga and Associates, *Four Stages of Life* (San Francisco: Jossey-Bass Publishers, 1975), p. 244.

9. M. Powell Lawton and Bonnie Simon, "The Ecology of Social Relationships in Housing for the Elderly," *The Gerontologist*, vol. 8 (1968), pp. 108–9.

APPENDIX A

Quantitative Procedures Employed in the Study

In this appendix we will explain our statistical procedures in a way that allows those without technical background to follow the explanation. We ask the indulgence of those readers who are well-versed in statistical methods.

In an overview of the use of statistics, Wallace and Roberts suggest that almost everybody goes through two attitudinal stages in regard to statistical conclusions. The first stage is a generally uncritical acceptance: "In discussion or argument, we wilt the first time somebody quotes statistics, or even asserts that he has seen some."[1] However, since most of us have had the experience of being misled by the glib but dubious use of statistics, many come in the second stage to distrust them and reject them out of hand. We trust that in following the course of our analysis, readers will take a position between these two extremes. We do not expect readers to approach our analysis uncritically, but at the same time we hope that they will be sympathetic to our particular use of statistics as a tool in understanding this complex subject of life satisfaction. For as Wallace and Roberts conclude: "Statistics, when used effectively, becomes so intertwined in the whole fabric of the subject to which it is applied as to be an integral part of it. Full appreciation of the ways in which statistics enters into an investigation requires, therefore, a detailed analysis of the subject matter and of all the methods brought to bear on it."[2]

The first statistical procedure we would like to discuss is used in relation to the indices described on pages 39-45. To construct these indices, we combined in an additive fashion those interview responses appropriate to a given concept (index) to produce for each person in our sample a score for each index. For an example of an index, see Appendix B.1. There are two major questions associated with the construction of indices. First, does each item in the index contribute to the measurement of what the index as a whole purports to measure? In other words, is the index unidimensional? Second, can the index score be obtained legitimately by adding the value of one item to the value of other items? In other words, is the index cumulative? One statistical procedure which enables the researcher to determine whether or not these questions can be answered in the affirmative is Guttman scale analysis. By constructing a matrix with one dimension being the order in which respondents are ranked by index scores, and the other dimension being the order in which index items are ranked according to their "degree of difficulty" (i.e., according to the proportion of the sample which passed or failed—selected or rejected— them), Guttman scaling determines the extent to which a set of items is both unidimensional and cumulative. We have applied Guttman scale analysis to the various sets of items which constitute our indices. All of the indices used in our analysis approximate (have less than 10 percent errors) the ideal Guttman scale and have a coefficient scalability greater than 0.6. In the ideal Guttman scale, a respondent who passes a more difficult item will not have failed a less difficult item, and each person's responses can be predicted from his rank alone.[3]

The variables included in our analysis—that are not indices—are either based on interval data or on dichotomous responses. These latter "nominal" variables have no intrinsic value and are assigned arbitrary values. For example, in regard to the variable SEX, males were assigned the value "0" and females the value "1." However, since the distance between two such arbitrary values is known, nominal variables may be, and in our analysis are, treated as though they were based on interval data.[4]

In observing the distributions of the variables in our data set, we found that most variables approached normal distribution; that is, they were not bimodal distributions nor did they have extreme kurtosis in either the positive or negative direction. In a few cases, we collapsed two categories to achieve more normal distribution. This was done without violating the integrity of the measure (i.e., the intent of the question). Some variables were skewed, though none extremely so. However, to be certain that these variables did not produce spurious associations because of non-normality, we measured the correlations among the variables by both a parametric (Pearson's "r") and a non-parametric (Kendall's Tau) statistic.[5] The results of the two procedures were so similar we were able to conclude that use of parametric statistics would not yield spurious findings. Further, if there was any doubt concerning the linearity of given relationships, we used the Base 10 logarithmic values of relevant variables in the same analysis and by comparing results concluded that in these given instances exponentially curvelinear relationships did not obtain.

Each of the variables in our analysis is in turn treated as a dependent variable. In order to determine the combination of all remaining variables which best explains or predicts each of the dependent variables, we use stepwise multiple regression analysis. For our purposes, the most important products of this analysis are the standardized multiple regression coefficients (betas) and the "variance explained" by the combination of independent variables. Theoretically betas range from -1.0 through 0 to +1.0. They measure the strength of the relationship between each of the independent variables (among the "combination" of variables) and a given dependent variable, when all the other independent variables in the "combination" are held constant. The closer a beta approaches 1 in either direction, the stronger is that relationship. The explained variance is operationally defined as the multiple correlation coefficient squared.

There are two other products of multiple regression analysis that are important to our study: the residual and the F ratio. The residual is operationally defined as the square root of (1.0 minus the explained variance), or:

$$Res = 1 - Mult\ R^2$$

The F ratio is operationally defined as the mean square explained by the entire regression equation, divided by the mean square of the residuals, or:

$$F = \frac{MS\ reg}{MS\ res}$$

Essentially, the F ratio measures the extent to which the relationship between an independent and dependent variable is statistically significant beyond mere chance. In our analysis, to be included in the combination of variables "explaining" MORALE and PERSONAL SATISFACTION an independent variable must be significantly related to these dependent variables at the .01 level. For the moment, let us consider as "primary" the direct relationships between independent variables and MORALE, and all other relationships as "secondary." The inclusion criterion for all secondary relationships is that an independent variable must contribute 1 percent or more to the total explained variance. We decided on this more restrictive criterion in order to limit the number of variables to the most significant and thereby achieve as much clarity as possible in the exceedingly complex network of secondary relationships.

Up to this point we have been talking about a network of relationships leading to life satisfaction. Now we have arrived at the place where it is necessary to make this rather loose construct more explicit in terms of a systematic quantitative procedure. By adhering to certain assumptions, an investigator may utilize multiple regression analysis to develop what is known as a "path analysis" which assigns directions to relationships among variables. "Path analysis is not a procedure for demonstrating causality. [Rather,] it is a method for tracing out the implications of a set of causal assumptions which the researcher is willing to impose upon a system of relationships."[6] Our analysis entails the development of path models in which the two underlying assumptions are weak causal ordering and causal closure. In the first instance, we assume that the variables in the models for theoretical reasons or because of logical temporal sequences have been assigned proper positions in a causal chain. In the second instance, it is assumed that causal relationships in the models are closed to outside influence. This assumption is met by including a latent variable in the model that represents all of the model's unexplained variance. This latent variable is the residual described above and because of its inclusion, all variance is accounted for in a given model. If an investigator arbitrarily removes a variable from the causal chain, its influence does not just disappear but becomes manifest in the increased size of the residual. (Residuals are not included in our graphic models but appear in Appendix C.)

Thus, our analysis involves the construction of models consisting of hypothesized causal relationships that are tested through stepwise multiple regression and that are subject to the assumptions discussed above. In constructing the models, the direction of relationship between certain pairs of variables is apparent. For example, the sex of respondents may, or may not, affect their level of activity, but there is no way that their level of activity can affect their sex. A somewhat less obvious example is that the extent of a respondent's formal education may, or may not, influence his attitude about being with other people; and if we were referring to a sample of much younger people, the reverse also would be true. But for virtually our entire sample of elderly people, formal schooling is a thing of the past. Therefore, we can assume that one's attitude about being with people will not affect the extent of one's formal education. Since the incomes of people in our sample are relatively "fixed," the same logic would apply to that variable, and to others as well.

There are relationships between pairs of variables for which there are no compelling theoretical or temporal bases for positing causal direction. In order to include such relationships in the analysis, it was necessary to establish some logical and consistent criterion for assigning direction to them. Our solution to this problem may at first seem somewhat convoluted, but in fact it is a rather straightforward and logical procedure. We first ran stepwise multiple regression analyses without imposing the assumptions of path analysis. Each variable in our data set was treated, in turn, as the dependent variable, with all remaining variables in the data set treated as independent variables. If variable X appeared as one of the variables significantly influencing dependent variable Y, but variable Y did not appear as one of the variables significantly influencing dependent variable X, we posited a causal direction from X to Y. If both variables had a statistically significant impact on each other, their relationship was entered in the model as being "ambiguous;" that is, no causal direction would be attributed to the relationship.[7] One would expect a variable that measures a general attitude toward life, namely MORALE, to have an influence on a variety of other variables, and our regression analysis confirms this expectation. Since the purpose of this study is to explore the determinants of life satisfaction, MORALE as an independent variable has been excluded from the path analyses. Thus, its influence on other dependent variables is accounted for in the residual.[8]

Once all hypothetical causal relationships were established, a new series of stepwise multiple regression analyses were run; this time the independent variables were limited to those that had been hypothesized as impacting on the dependent variable under consideration, and this time the assumptions of weak causal ordering and closure were in effect.

Notes

1. W. Allen Wallace and Harry V. Roberts, *The Nature of Statistics* (New York: Free Press, 1962), p. 29.

2. *Ibid.*, p. 43.

3. In Guttman's terms a set of items constitutes a scale if, ". . . it is possible to derive from the population distribution a quantitative variable (scale) with which to characterize the population, such that each attribute (item) is a simple function of that quantitative variable (scale)." L. Guttman, "A Basis for Scaling Qualitative Data," *American Sociological Review*, vol. 9 (1944), pp. 139–50.

4. Nominal variables in our data set include the following: EMPLOYMENT, RACE, MARITAL STATUS, KC AREA CHILDREN, and SEX.

5. Non-parametric statistics do not assume a particular distribution in the population and for this reason are sometimes referred to as "distribution free" statistics.

6. In Norman H. Nie, C. Hadlai Hull, Jean G. Jenkins, Karin Steinbrenner, and Dale H. Bent, *Statistical Package for the Social Sciences* (New York: McGraw Hill, 1975), p. 389.

7. Of course, even this procedure does not assure that directionality has been definitely determined since the negative results would apply only to this specific data set.

8. In the context of this analysis, we conceive of MORALE as a manifestation of mental health, which dictates its designation as a dependent variable.

APPENDIX B

1. Responses from which the CAPACITY Index was created: All items passed the Guttman Scale analysis.

   Here are some tasks which you may or may not do, but could you do them without difficulty, or would you need help?

COULD DO MYSELF	WOULD NEED HELP	
[1]	[2]	Making the bed
[1]	[2]	Preparing a hot meal
[1]	[2]	Sweeping or vacuuming
[1]	[2]	Carrying out the garbage
[1]	[2]	Doing the laundry
[1]	[2]	Shopping for groceries
[1]	[2]	Washing the windows
[1]	[2]	Mowing the lawn
[1]	[2]	Shoveling snow

2. Responses from which the MORALE Index was created. An asterisk denotes individual items that "scaled" according to the Guttman Scale analysis.

For the next few questions I would simply like to know how you feel in general.

*First, how satisfied are you with your life today?

[3] SATISFIED   [2] NOT SURE   [1] DISSATISFIED

Do you often feel moody and blue?

[1] OFTEN   [2] SOMETIMES   [3] SELDOM, OR NEVER

*How have your spirits been lately?

[3] GOOD   [2] SO-SO   [1] POOR

How often do you get the feeling that your life today is not very useful?

[1] OFTEN   [2] SOMETIMES   [3] SELDOM, OR NEVER

Are you less interested in things like your personal appearance, table manners, and things like that?

[1] YES   [2] NOT SURE   [3] NO

*How much do you plan ahead the things you will be doing next week or the week after?

[3] A GOOD DEAL   [2] NOT SURE   [1] VERY LITTLE

*Have you felt lately that life is not worth living?

[1] YES   [2] NOT SURE   [3] NO

*How much happiness would you say you find in life today?

[3] A GOOD DEAL   [2] ABOUT AS MUCH AS CAN BE EXPECTED   [1] LITTLE OR NONE

3. ABILITY TO COPE WITH PROBLEMS Index, including only those items that passed the Guttman Scale analysis.

Are there any social services provided in this area that you have used in the past year [including Kansas City, Missouri]?

[1] YES   specify

[2] NO

Are you aware of any group or agency that could help you if you had a complaint against some store or salesman?

[1] YES   specify

[2] NO

If you were to need legal assistance, where would you go for help?

[1] private lawyer or legal aid society

[2] police, church, or welfare agency

[3] I wouldn't know where to go

[4] Other response   specify

Do you have any medical, surgical, or hospital insurance now?

[1] YES

[2] NO

APPENDIX C

Variance Explained and Residual for Dependent Variables

Dependent Variable	Variance Explained	Residual
Morale	.27	.85
Cond. of Neigh.	.14	.93
Activity	.17	.91
Income Adequacy	.34	.81
Ability to Cope	.21	.89
Auto Ownership	.32	.82
% Elderly	.07	.96
Social Attitude	.05	.97
Marital Status	.18	.90
Dep. on Family	.44	.75
Dep. on Fr. & Neigh.	.43	.76
Public Transport.	.20	.89
Religiosity	.12	.94
Self Transport.	.56	.66
Capacity	.09	.95

Bibliography

Atchley, Robert C. *The Social Forces in Later Life: An Introduction to Social Gerontology*. Belmont, Cal.: Wadsworth, 1972.

Aucoin, Jackie, and C. Neil Bull. "Voluntary Association Participation and Life Satisfaction: A Replication Note," *Journal of Gerontology*, vol. 30, no. 1 (1975), 73–76.

Bateson, Gregory. *Steps to an Ecology of Mind*. New York: Ballantine Books, 1972.

Berghorn, Forrest J., and Ronald C. Naugle. *Changing Residence in Kansas City, Kansas: The Geographic and Socioeconomic Bases of Urban Mobility*. Kansas City, Kan.: Mid-America Urban Observatory, 1973.

Berkhofer, Robert F., Jr. *A Behavioral Approach to Historical Analysis*. New York: The Free Press, 1969.

Bild, Bernice R., and Robert J. Havighurst. "Senior Citizens in Great Cities: The Case of Chicago," *The Gerontologist*, vol. 11, Part II (February, 1976), 3–88.

Billingsley, Andrew. *Black Families in White America*. Englewood Cliffs, N.J.: Prentice-Hall, 1968.

Bloom, Larry, B. Kent Houston, David S. Holmes, and Thomas G. Burish. "The Effectiveness of Attentual Diversion and Situation Redefinition for Reducing Stress Due to a Nonambiguous Threat," *Journal of Research in Personality*, vol. 11 (1977), 83–94.

Booth, Alan. "Sex and Social Participation," *American Sociological Review*, vol. 37 (April, 1972), 183–92.

Borgatta, Edgar F., and Charles F. Westoff. "The Prediction of Total Fertility," *Milbank Memorial Fund Quarterly*, vol. 32 (October, 1954), 383–419.

Bultena, Gordon L., and Vivian Wood. "The American Retirement Community: Bane or Blessing?" Paper presented at the annual meeting of the American Sociological Association, Denver, 1968.

Butler, Robert N. *Why Survive? Being Old in America*. New York: Harper & Row, 1975.

Cameron, Paul. "Ego Strength and Happiness of the Aged," *Journal of Gerontology*, vol. 22 (April, 1967), 199-202.

———— , et al. "Personality Differences Between Typical Urban Negroes and Whites," *Journal of Negro Education*, vol. 40 (1971), 66-75.

———— , et al. "The Life Satisfaction of Nonnormal Persons," *Journal of Consulting and Clinical Psychology*, vol. 41, no. 2 (1973), 207-14.

Campbell, Angus. "Aspirations, Satisfaction and Fulfillment," in Angus Campbell and Philip Converse, eds., *The Human Meaning of Social Change*. New York: Russell Sage Foundation, 1972.

Cantilli, E. J., and J. L. Schmelzer, eds. *Transportation and Aging*. Washington, D.C.: U.S. Government Printing Office, 1971, 100-107.

Carp, Frances M. "Correlates of Mobility Among Retired Persons," *EDRA Two: Proceedings of the Second Annual Environmental Design Research Association Converence* (October), 1970, 171-82.

————. "Public Transit and Retired People," in E. J. Cantilli and J. L. Schmelzer, eds., *Transportation and Aging: Selected Issues*. Washington, D.C.: U.S. Government Printing Office, 1971, 82-92.

————. "The Mobility of Retired People," in Cantilli and Schmelzer, *op. cit.*, 1971, 23-41.

————. "Retired People as Automobile Passengers," *Gerontologist*, vol. 12 (Spring, 1972), 67-72.

Clark, Margaret, and Barbara G. Anderson. *Culture and Aging*. Springfield, Ill.: Charles C. Thomas, 1967.

————. "Cultural Values and Dependence in Later Life," in Donald O. Cowgill and Lowell D. Holmes, eds., *Aging and Modernization*. New York: Appleton-Century-Crofts, 1972.

Clemente, Frank, and William J. Sauer. "Life Satisfaction in the United States," *Social Forces*, vol. 54 (March, 1976), 621-31.

Coelho, George V., David Hamburg, and John E. Adams. "Synthesis of Biological and Social Perspectives," in Coelho, *et al.*, eds., *Coping and Adaptation*. New York: Basic Books, Inc., 1974.

Cumming, Elaine, and William E. Henry. *Growing Old: The Process of Disengagement*. New York: Basic Books, 1961.

Cutler, Stephen J. "Voluntary Association Participation and Life Satisfaction: A Cautionary Research Note," *Journal of Gerontology*, vol. 28, no. 1 (1973), 96-100.

————. "The Effects of Transportation and Distance on Voluntary Association Participation Among the Aged," *International Journal on Aging and Human Development*, vol. 5, no. 1 (1974), 81-94.

Dubin, Robert. *Theory Building*. New York: Free Press, 1969.

Edwards, John N., and David L. Klemmack. "Correlates of Life Satisfaction: A Re-examination," *Journal of Gerontology*, vol. 28, no. 4 (1973), 497–502.

Frankl, Victor. *The Doctor and the Soul*. New York: Alfred A. Knopf, 1962.

Gal, Reuven, and Richard Lazarus. "The Role of Activity in Anticipating and Confronting Stressful Situations," in Coelho, *et al., op. cit.,* 1974.

Gans, Herbert J. "Planning and Social Life: Friendship and Neighbor Relations in Suburban Communities," *Journal of the American Institute of Planners*, vol. 27 (May, 1961), 134–40.

Garrison, William L. "Limitations and Constraints of Existing Transportation Systems as Applied to the Elderly," in E. G. Cantilli and J. L. Schmelzer, eds., *Transportation and Aging*, Washington, D.C.: U.S. Government Printing Office, 1971, 100–07.

Gubrium, Jaber F. "Apprehensions of Coping Incompetence and Responses to Fear in Old Age," *International Journal of Aging and Human Development*, vol. 4 (Spring, 1973), 111–23.

——. *The Myth of the Golden Years*. Springfield, Ill.: Charles C. Thomas, 1973.

Guttman, L. "A Basis for Scaling Qualitative Data," *American Sociological Review*, vol. 9 (1944), 139–50.

Hall, Edward T. *The Silent Language*. New York: Doubleday, 1973.

Harris, Louis, and Associates, Inc. *The Myth and Reality of Aging in America*. Washington, D.C.: National Council on Aging, Inc., 1975.

Havighurst, Robert, J., and Ruth Albrecht. *Older People*. New York: Longmans, Green & Co., 1953.

Hess, Beth. "Friendship," in Matilda White Riley *et al.*, eds., *A Sociology of Age Stratification*, vol. 3 of "Aging and Society." New York: Russell Sage Foundation, 1972. Pp. 357–93.

Holmes, David S. "Compensation for Ego Threat: Two Experiments," *Journal of Personality and Social Psychology*, vol. 18 (1973), 234–37.

—— and B. Kent Houston. "Effectiveness of Situation Redefinition and Affective Isolation in Coping with Stress," *Journal of Personality and Social Psychology*, vol. 29 (1974), 212–18.

Hsu, Francis L. K. "American Core Value and National Character," in F. L. K. Hsu, ed., *Psychological Anthropology: Approaches to Culture and Personality*. Homewood, Ill.: Dorsey, 1961, 209–30.

Kerckhoff, Alan C. "Family Patterns and Morale in Retirement," in Ida H. Simpson and John C. McKinney, eds., *Social Aspects of Aging*. Durham, N.C.: Duke University Press, 1966, 173–94.

Kiser, Clyde, and Pascal K. Whelpton. "Summary of Chief Findings and

Implications for Future Studies," *Milbank Memorial Fund Quarterly*, vol. 36 (July 1958), 282–329.

Kutner, Bernard, David Fanshel, Alice Togo, and Thomas S. Langner. *Five Hundred Over Sixty: A Community Survey on Aging*. New York: Russell Sage Foundation, 1956.

Lawton, M. Powell, and Bonnie Simon. "The Ecology of Social Relationships in Housing for the Elderly," *The Gerontologist*, vol. 8 (1968), 108–15.

Lazarsfeld, Paul F., and Robert K. Merton. "Friendship as Social Process: A Substantive and Methodological Analysis," in Morroe Berger, Theodore Abel, and Charles H. Page, eds., *Freedom and Control in Modern Society*. New York: D. Van Nostrand Co., 1954, 18–66.

Lemon, Bruce W., Vern L. Bengtson, and James A. Peterson. "An Exploration of the Activity Theory of Aging: Activity Types and Life Satisfaction Among In-Movers to a Retirement Community," *Journal of Gerontology*, vol. 27 (1972), 511–23.

Lohmann, Nancy. "Correlates of Life Satisfaction, Morale and Adjustment Measures," *Journal of Gerontology*, vol. 32 (1977), 73–75.

Lopata, Helena Z. "The Social Involvement of American Widows," *American Behavioral Scientist*, vol. 14 (1970), 41–57.

——— . "Role Changes in Widowhood: A World Perspective," in Donald O. Cowgill and Lowell D. Holmes, eds., *Aging and Modernization*. New York: Appleton-Century-Crofts, 1972.

Lowenthal, Marjorie Fiske, Majda Thurnher, David Chiriboga and Associates. *Four Stages of Life*. San Francisco: Jossey-Bass Publishers, 1975.

Maddox, George L. "Activity and Morale: A Longitudinal Study of Selected Elderly Subjects," *Social Forces*, vol. 42 (1963), 195–204.

Mandelbaum, Seymour J. *Community and Communications*. New York: W. W. Norton and Co., Inc., 1972.

Marble, Duane, Perry O. Hanson, and Susan H. Hanson. "Intraurban Mobility Patterns of Elderly Households: A Swedish Example," *Proceedings of the Transportation Research Forum, First Conference on Transportation*. Bruges, Belgium, 1973. 655–66.

Markovitz, Joni. "The Transportation Needs of the Elderly," in E. J. Cantilli and J. L. Schmelzer, eds., *Transportation and Aging*. Washington, D.C.: U.S. Government Printing Office, 1971, 67–81.

Messer, Mark. "The Possibility of American Age-Concentrated Environment Becoming a Normative System," *The Gerontologist*, vol. 7 (1967), 247–50.

——— . "Age Grouping and the Family Status of the Elderly," *Sociology and Social Research*, vol. 52 (1968), 271–79.

Moss, Walter, and Gordon. *Growing Old*. New York: Pocket Books, 1975.

Murphy, Gardner. *Personality: A Bio-Social Approach to Origins and Structure.* New York: Harper & Brothers, 1947. Chapter 8.

Nye, Norman H., C. Hadlai Hull, Jean G. Jenkins, Karin Steinbrenner, and Dale H. Bent. *Statistical Package for the Social Sciences.* New York: McGraw-Hill Book Co., 1975.

Orbach, Harold L. "The Disengagement Theory of Aging, 1960-1970: A Case Study of Scientific Controversy." Ph.D. Dissertation, University of Minnesota, 1974.

Palmore, E., and C. Luikart. "Health and Social Factors Related to Life Satisfaction," *Journal of Health and Social Behavior* (1972), 68–70.

Philadelphia City Planning Commission. *Locational Criteria for Housing for the Elderly,* Internal Report, December, 1968.

Pignataro, Louis J. "Introduction," in E. J. Cantilli and J. L. Schmelzer, eds., *Transportation and Aging.* Washington, D.C.: U.S. Government Printing Office, 1971, 3–6.

Planning Department. "Historical Profile," Kansas City, Kan.: Community Renewal Program, 1969.

Poorkaj, Houshang. "Social-Psychological Factors and 'Successful Aging,' " *Sociology and Social Research,* vol. 56 (April, 1972), 289–300.

Rose, Arnold M., and Warren A. Peterson, eds. *Older People and Their Social World: The Sub-Culture of the Aging.* Philadelphia: F. A. Davis Company, 1965.

Rosenfelt, Rosalie H. "The Elderly Mystique," *Journal of Social Issues,* vol. 21 (1965), 37–43.

Rosow, Irving. *Social Integration of the Aged.* New York: Free Press, 1967.

——— . "Old People, Their Friends and Neighbors," *American Behavioral Scientist,* vol. 14 (Spring, 1970), 59–69.

Shanas, Ethel. "Family Responsibility and the Health of Older People," *Journal of Gerontology,* vol. 15 (October, 1960), 408–11.

Spreitzer, Elmer, and Eldon E. Snyder. "Correlates of Life Satisfaction Among the Aged," *Journal of Gerontology,* vol. 29 (1974), 454–58.

Srole, Leo. "Social Integration and Certain Corollaries: An Exploratory Study," *American Sociological Review,* vol. 21 (1956), 709–16.

Streib, Gordon F. "Intergenerational Relations: Perspectives of the Two Generations on the Older Parent," *Journal of Marriage and the Family,* vol. 27 (November, 1965), 469–76.

——— . "Old Age and the Family," *American Behavioral Scientist,* vol. 14 (Spring, 1970), 25–39.

——— . "Retirement: Crisis or Continuities?" in Carter C. Osterbind, ed., *Migration, Mobility and Aging.* Gainesville: Center for Gerontological Studies and Programs, University of Florida, 1975, 21–41.

Tibbits, Clark, ed. *Handbook of Social Gerontology*. Chicago: University of Chicago Press, 1960.

Tissue, Thomas. "Another Look at Self-Rated Health Among the Elderly," *Journal of Gerontology*, vol. 27 (January, 1974), 91–94.

Trueblood, Elton D. *The Life We Prize*. New York: Harper & Brothers, 1951.

Wallace, W. Allen, and Harry V. Roberts. *The Nature of Statistics*. New York: Free Press, 1962.

Watzlawick, Paul, *et al. Change: Principles of Problem Formation and Problem Resolution*. New York: W. W. Norton, 1973.

Weiss, Robert S. "The Fund of Sociability," in Helena Z. Lopata, ed., *Marriages and Family*. New York: Van Nostrand, 1973.

Woodring, Paul. "Why 65? The Case Against Mandatory Retirement," *Saturday Review* (August, 1976), 18–20.

Wynn, F. Houston, and Herbert S. Levinson. "Some Considerations in Appraising Bus Transit Potentials," *Highway Research Record, No. 197: Passenger Transportation*, Highway Research Board, NRC, 1967, 1–24.

Index